WORKING FROM HOME

in **90** Minutes

Alan Dixie FICM

2000

Copyright © Alan Dixie 2008

First published in 2007 by Management Books 2000 Ltd
Forge House, Limes Road
Kemble, Cirencester
Gloucestershire, GL7 6AD, UK
Tel: 0044 (0) 1285 771441
Fax: 0044 (0) 1285 771055
Email: info@mb2000.com
Web: www.mb2000.com

British Library Cataloguing in Publication Data is available

ISBN 9781852525866

Contents

Introduction 9

1. The Office in the Home 13
   The required building blocks.................................. 13

2. The Advantages of Home-Working for the Company 22
   Benefits for the employer.................................. 22

3. The Advantages of Home-Working for the Employee 29
   Benefits for the employee 29

4. Other Advantages of Home-Working..................................... 35
   Our carbon footprint..................................... 35
   Reducing those greenhouse gases 36
   Reducing the drain on the NHS................................ 37
   Regeneration of the local community........................... 37
   Reduced traffic flow 37

5. Managing the Home-Worker 39
   Well-maintained equipment................................ 40
   Controlled workflow..................................... 40
   No man is an island..................................... 41
   Office-based support 41
   Out of sight, out of mind................................. 42
   Managing through performance targets 42

6. Developing a Home-Working System 45
   Maslow's motivational categories 47
   Invasion of the home-wreckers.............................. 50
   Do not over-analyse 50
   A truly remarkable system................................ 51

7. Measuring Performance **53**
Define what you are trying to achieve............................ *54*
Isolate the definitive elements *54*
Setting targets to increase productivity......................... *55*
Using the system to measure performance...................... *55*

8. Evaluating the Successful Results **61**
Increased working hours.. *61*
The setting of clear goals *63*
Creating a competitive edge.. *68*
Creating a good team spirit *69*

9. The Whole Truth and Nothing *But* the Truth **71**
Mine.. *72*
Michael... *73*
Sam.. *74*
Diane... *75*
Amanda *76*
Paul *78*
The manager's perspective... *79*
Kevin's story... *80*
Conclusions *81*

10. Revisiting the Obsolete Office Survey **83**
Rating the benefits... *83*
Rating the disadvantages *84*
Improved working conditions.. *84*

11. The British Telecom Survey **87**
The British Telecom system... *87*
E-Working at BT *88*
Conferencing at BT *89*

12. The Greater Perspective **91**
Crossrail... *92*
Increasing capacity by driving on the hard shoulder of
    motorways *93*
The increasing population of Britain *95*

Contents

13. Health & Safety Executive Guide to Home-Working 97

What the law requires 97

How to do a risk assessment 98

Some common hazards... 100

Using work equipment at home................................. 101

Using electrical equipment for home-working.......... 102

Working with VDUs 103

New and expectant mothers....................................... 105

Reporting of Injuries, Disease & Dangerous Occurrences

*   Regulations 1995 (RIDDOR 95) 105*

Health & Safety Executive inspectors 105

Further information.. 106

14. Sample Contract 107

Amendment to general terms and conditions of employment for

*   home-based employees... 108*

Public sector, local government and utilities........... 111

Other companies' contracts 114

Conclusions 121

Index 125

7

Introduction

"Working from home, are you serious?"

"Pay people for sitting at home doing nothing, you must be joking!"

"It's a great idea in principle, but of course it will never work for *our* staff."

I wish I had a pound for every time I have heard those lines – thoughtless reactions from short-sighted managers that slip so easily off the tongue. Lines designed to hide the speaker's lack of knowledge or understanding of home-based working, and the benefits it can bring to an organisation. So forgive me for taking this chance to get my revenge, but yes I am serious. No, I'm not joking. And yes it does work, even for *your* workers. *Working From Home in 90 Minutes* explains how the process works, and shows how it helps both individuals and organisations to increase productivity, reduce costs, and dramatically increase job satisfaction.

Rather than glibly dismiss home-working, managers should be asking what it can do for them, and why they need to embrace it. That's the big question that we should *all* be asking – and hopefully by the time you finish this book you will have the answer.

So let's start a journey of discovery, and look at some of the reasons for implementing home-based working.

Reason 1. Because it's good for the environment and would help to reduce our carbon footprint.

This benefit is definitely important, but I would question whether the majority of businesses (particularly the bigger ones) really care

9

enough about the environment for this reason to carry much weight on its own.

Reason 2. Because it's good for our staff, and enables them to live a more balanced, and less stressed life. After all, a healthy workforce is a productive work force, not to mention less of a burden on the National Health Service.

Once again this is another valid statement, and another important reason why we should embrace home-working. However, even this reason, which offers a direct benefit to the company through reduced absenteeism, is not the reason why large corporations will eventually implement home-based working.

Reason 3. Probably the least noble of all, but without doubt the only reason home-based working will grow substantially over the next decade, is purely a financial one. Home-based working will allow companies to increase their productivity by up to 100 per cent, while at the same time cutting their overhead costs and substantially increasing their profits.

As I will demonstrate in this book, these benefits are real, and this is the reason that home-working is already growing rapidly in the business community. The financial argument for home-working is undeniable, and managers will ignore it at their peril.

There is nothing mystical about home-working. You don't need to be an I.T. expert or some kind of management guru; you simply need to get past the trust issue and learn how to manage a remote worker. I can say without fear of contradiction that this book will deliver everything you need to know – a simple process that will enable you to implement and manage a successful home-working process. There is no smoke, no mirrors, and no illusion, just a tried and tested managerial process backed up by common sense and trust.

It is seven years since I wrote my first book on home-working, *The Obsolete Office*, and the world has changed a lot in that time. People are now beginning to realise the benefits that home-based working brings – benefits for both the employer and the employee.

Working From Home in 90 Minutes has been written as an easy-to-follow guide that will lead the reader through the processes of implementing home-based working, a guide that will take you from conception to profit. Unlike other books written on this subject, this book will also provide the proof that you can turn the dream into reality. You will hear from actual home-based workers and managers, hear first-hand how you can work harder yet feel less stressed, how you can be more productive yet enjoy more leisure time. And last but not least, how to offer your employees more freedom but have more managerial control.

It's time to join the revolution and move on to a new way of working, to use modern technology to change our lives for the better. We need to change our concept of work from something we go to, to something that comes to us. This book will lead you to a new working process that will help to increase profits, play an important part in improving the environment, and offer employees a healthier lifestyle. So fasten your seatbelts and enjoy the ride, for going to work will never be the same again.

1

The Office in the Home

Even the most impressive skyscrapers are built from solid foundations and the same is also true of any effective business processes. Therefore, before we get involved in the more glamorous areas of managing home-based workers, or the financial benefits that home-working brings, let's take a closer look at those all-important foundation stones.

The required building blocks

- A broadband telephone line
- A Starfax number
- A computer
- A printer
- A desk and chair
- Your own space

A broadband telephone line

This is your lifeline to the outside world, the umbilical cord that connects you to your office and your fellow workers. A broadband line will vary in speed dependant on the supplier of your service, but even the slowest service will be powerful enough to meet your requirements. My home-workers certainly do not find any deterioration in the speed of their operating system.

13

You will access your works computer through a secure VPN (Virtual Private Network) connection that allows a two-way transfer of data. This will offer a secure password-controlled operating platform, while your company's firewall will prevent any viruses attacking the company's main computer systems.

Installing a broadband line is a very simple process; however, there are a few points that you need to remember before ordering the installation.

1. You should always install a *business* broadband line because service providers such as British Telecom will give priority to service calls logged by a business user. They will usually repair faults on business users' lines within 24 hours of the initial fault report; unfortunately the same is not true for personal subscriber lines. It is also important to find a reliable supplier, which may not always be the cheapest, as interruptions to supply will cause problems and reduce productivity.

2. The business broadband line should be set up in the name of your company and not your personal name, as the latter could leave you open to a tax liability with the broadband line being seen as a benefit in kind. You should also make sure that all passwords and security codes are held on file by the I.T. department, as they will be needed if you need to contact the service provider to log a fault.

3. It is advisable to have a separate broadband line for personal use, as this avoids any confusion regarding the company's responsibility for payment of the business account. There is nothing worse than trawling through an itemised bill trying to work out which charge is work-related and which relates to personal use. I would also strongly advise that broadband bills are paid by direct debit. I speak from personal experience here, and can assure you that some of the larger service providers have trouble matching other payment methods to actual invoices, which can lead to services being mistakenly disconnected.

14

A Starfax number

One of the most important things when working from home is not to clutter your house with unnecessary equipment. The office needs to fit harmoniously into the home, not take it over. If you don't get this right you will soon get complaints from other members of the household. One of the most important benefits of home-working is working in a less stressed environment, and you should avoid undermining this benefit by upsetting other members of the household.

With the above in mind, subscribing to a service like Starfax is essential. This type of system will allow you to send and receive faxes from your computer without the need for a scanner or fax machine, both of which tend to be bulky items that take up a lot of office space. The Starfax service will turn any fax that is sent to your Starfax number into an email, which is then forwarded to your computer. Likewise, it will also turn an email you send into a fax and forward it to the recipient's fax number. This has proved to be a very useful service, and one that we at Centaur have also installed for all our office-based workers. By using a Starfax system you never need to lose another fax, as a copy is always held on your computer. The image quality of the Starfax document will also be superior when compared to the printed copy received from most fax machines.

A computer

Your computer will obviously be the hub of all your home-working activity, and it is important to get the set-up right, from the start. You don't want the computer to be too obtrusive, especially if you use the living room or dining room as your office. So, despite what you may have heard, size does matter, and that is why we have supplied our home-workers with very small Dell computers and flat-screen monitors. The smaller the computer, the less it will dominate a room, and the same is also true when using a flat screen monitor. However, if you are working on a tight budget any Internet-ready computer will suffice.

15

If you do not have a spare room that you can utilise as an office, and wish to pack the office away completely at the end of the day, the best option would be to use a laptop, although I would suggest using one with a full-sized keyboard. However, it should be remembered that laptops are less reliable than desktop computers, and your aim should always be to keep computer malfunctions to a minimum – it goes without saying that frequent crashes and reboots cost time and money, and any longer-term faults can have a serious impact on productivity.

As referred to above, your computer should be connected to the office network via a VPN set-up. When you work from home your computer simply acts as a dumb terminal, and has no real effect on processing speed. The speed of your system rests solely with the bandwidth and traffic levels through the company's Internet connection, and the speed of the office-based servers, which is where all the computing power comes from. (See Fig1:1) This type of set-up means that there is no need to purchase the fastest and most powerful computer when you initiate home-based working; it is far more important to find equipment that will fit best in the home-based office.

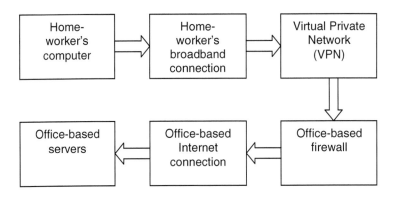

Fig 1:1 Home-based data flow

Home-workers using this kind of system do not have to worry about losing their work if their computer crashes, as it will be saved on a company network drive and not the local hard drive in their computer. All companies should back up their network drives each night so important data will not get lost or corrupted through a computer malfunction.

Another benefit of saving your work on a network drive is that you can access all your files whether you are logged in from home or using a computer at work.

An additional advantage of using a laptop, which may outweigh the fact that they are less reliable, is that you can take it with you when you need to visit the office. This means that the work-based space can be better utilised because you do not need to keep spare workstations set up for your home-workers.

A printer

The type of printer you use will depend on the amount of space you have; unfortunately, even inkjet printers tend to be bulky. However, if you need to print high-quality documents, a laser printer may be required, but note that these are bulky items. In most circumstances a simple inkjet printer will be more than sufficient for your printing needs. Dot matrix printers should be avoided at all costs due to the level of operating noise they emit. Speaking from personal experience, I would also advise that you steer clear of all-in-one printer/scanner/copiers, as these products come with some fairly intricate software and can be very difficult to connect to a company's printer network.

A desk and chair

This is one area that does not get the attention it deserves, and if you don't get this set-up right it could cause health problems. Even when an employee works from home their company is still responsible for their **health and safety**. It is the employer's responsibility to ensure that all safety guidelines are adhered to, which means making sure that there are no electrical wires trailing across the floor, that any chair their home-worker uses meets current European Standards, and that their computer set-up meets the current ergonomic requirements. Working on a coffee table while sitting on the couch will definitely not suffice.

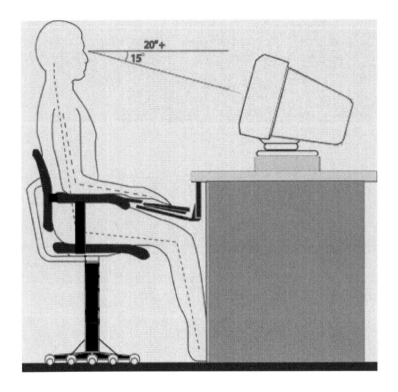

Fig 1:2 The correct ergonomic set-up for a workstation

A Quick Set-up Guide

If possible, your computer monitor should be positioned at right angles to any light source to minimise screen glare. The monitor should also be a reasonable distance away from you, but you should still be able to focus comfortably on the screen. A minimum distance of 20 inches should always be maintained. The height of the monitor should be adjusted so that the centre of the screen is slightly below eye level, approximately 15 degrees. I would also suggest using flat screen monitors where possible.

The office should be moderately lit with a mixture of incandescent and fluorescent lighting where possible. Avoid any harsh form of lighting and never use the monitor in the dark, as this will definitely cause eyestrain. Remember to look up from the screen at regular intervals and to focus on distant objects to avoid eyestrain. You should also take a short break every 20 minutes. Home-workers can easily get absorbed in what they are doing so it is important that they make a conscious effort to take these mini breaks.

The keyboard should be positioned slightly below the elbow allowing the wrists to remain straight, the neutral position. Although all keyboards come with supports to lift up the back of the keyboard these should not be used. The keyboard needs to remain flat to allow the wrists to remain in their neutral position when typing. It should also be remembered that wrist rests are designed for that purpose, to rest your wrists on; when typing, the wrists should naturally lift off the rest and take up their neutral position. Finally the keyboard should be kept in close proximity to the body; you should be able to reach the keys while your arms remain bent at the side of your body. If the keyboard is placed too far in front of you, your arms will have to stretch forward which is likely to cause pain in your shoulders, neck and upper back muscles. The mouse should be positioned next to the keyboard, once again in easy reach, so that you don't have to stretch to use it.

Your chair should have armrests, an adjustable lumbar support, and a height adjustment facility. The chair height should be adjusted so that your feet rest flat on the floor. The lumbar support should be set slightly below the waist line, and you should allow 1-3 inches between the edge of the seat and the back of your knees. If possible use a high-back chair that supports your shoulder blades.

Of course, the correct chair is of little use if you do not adopt the correct posture, so make sure that your hips are slightly higher than your knees and that your feet are flat on the floor. You should move your feet around from time to time, but never sit with your ankles crossed. Leaning back slightly in your seat will help to open up your hips and relieve the pressure on your pelvis. Your arms should hang naturally by your side and, as previously stated, your wrists should remain straight. Take 30-second micro-breaks every 20 minutes to refocus your eyes and reset your body position. Most of the people I see sitting at computers do not adopt the correct position, myself included, and I can speak from personal experience when I say that you will suffer unnecessarily if you don't. It may feel strange to start with but if you persevere in getting your body in the correct position it soon becomes a matter of habit.

I would also advise spending some of that money you have saved by not commuting to work on regular visits to an osteopath; this will help to maintain your body in good working order, reduce muscle strain, and hopefully prevent repetitive strain injury.

Your own space

Not everyone has the space to work from home; for example, if you live in a bedsit you will definitely struggle to meet the standard health and safety requirements. However, a separate room that you can dedicate as an office, while preferable, is not essential. I have managed members of staff who have worked successfully from the kitchen table, or a corner of the lounge. What is important is that you have somewhere to work that allows the proper set-up of equipment and is also free from distractions. It is impossible to work from the lounge if you have a two-year-old child running around, even if someone else is looking after them.

A spare bedroom or study that can be utilised as a dedicated office is obviously the ideal option. There are two primary reasons why this is true. Firstly, it is more conducive to work in an environment where you are less likely to be interrupted. Secondly, you also need to be able to mentally close the door on the office when the day is over. It is not healthy to let work dominate your life, and this can easily happen to the home-worker, so you need to find a way of mentally leaving the office. Shutting work behind the door of a room that you do not use for any other purpose is the most effective way of achieving this.

2

The Advantages of Home-Working for the Company

Do companies benefit from home-based working? You bet your life they do. Despite what some people will try to tell you, home-working definitely benefits both the employer and employee. Home-based working would never have taken its first breath if there were not something in it for everyone, and the fact that it is a growing phenomenon in itself proves all those doubters wrong. The benefits the employer will receive from introducing a home-based working system are now discussed in greater detail.

Benefits for the employer

- Increased productivity
- Reduced absenteeism levels
- Lower overhead costs
- Improved staff retention
- Reduced cost of commuting

Increased productivity

This is probably the most important benefit that the employer enjoys and is discussed in greater detail in Chapter 9, where I explain in full how to reduce employment costs and supply the facts and figures to prove that **working from home can increase**

productivity levels by up to 100 per cent. This increased productivity will enable the employer to reduce staffing levels, or alternatively, to cope with increased work levels without the need to increase staffing numbers. As any accountant will tell you, employment costs are the biggest drain on any company's profits and that is why increasing productivity is such an important benefit. The beauty of this benefit is that it is also totally scaleable, and therefore it is a true benefit to any size of business. The larger the department or company the greater the saving, as can be seen from the table in fig 2:1.

	Company		
	ABC Telesales	**One to One Telesales**	**Ultimate Telesales**
No of employees	10	30	50
Salary costs (£35,000 per employee)	£350,000	£1,050,000	£1,750,000
Employment costs (£17,500 per employee)	£175,000	£525,000	£875,000
Total costs	£525,000	£1,575,000	£2,625,000
Saving at 50% productivity increase	£175,000	£525,000	£875,000
Saving at 75% productivity increase	£225,000	£675,000	£1,125,000
Saving at 100% productivity increase	£262,500	£787,500	£1,312,500

Fig 2:1 Scalable employment costs through increased productivity

23

Reduced absenteeism levels

Reduced absenteeism is another benefit a company enjoys when implementing home-based working and there are basically two reasons for this reduction:

1. Reduced levels of work-related stress.

2. The ability to work through minor ailments at home that would otherwise incapacitate the office-based worker.

There is no doubt that stress plays a large part in the health of our employees. When a person is suffering from stress their productivity, and the quality of their work, will obviously be affected. But more importantly, stress creates a vicious circle of deterioration as it reduces the effectiveness of the body's immune system so that the individual concerned becomes less effective at fighting disease. An employee suffering in this way will suffer more often from ailments such as colds and flu. For those who suffer more prolonged bouts of stress, the ailments can be far more serious.

Work-related stress does not only relate to stress within the workplace. A lot of stress suffered by office-based workers is actually associated with their journey in to work. Being stuck for ages in your car, or on the underground in a claustrophobic tube carriage, places a large amount of stress on the body, stress that you cannot dissipate through the body's normal fight-or-flight reaction. The effects of this stress, the overproduction of adrenalin by the sympathetic nerves, remain in your body, tightening the muscles around the back and neck area, slowly transferring to the back of the head and finally across the forehead. Some people also experience a tightening of the chest muscles. Stress will make you feel tired and short tempered, not the best way to arrive at the office in the morning. All you need now is to be confronted by a couple of difficult problems when you arrive and you might as well write the whole day off, because as sure as eggs are eggs, it's not going to get any better.

Companies have a duty, under the *Management of Health and Safety at Work Regulations 1999*, to assess the risk of stress-related ill health arising from work activities; and under the *Health and Safety at Work Act 1974*, to take measures to control that risk. Implementing a home-working process is a way of meeting these obligations while at the same time increasing profitability.

Research carried out by the TUC suggests that stress at work costs employers £5bn a year. Approximately 13 million working days are lost to stress, depression and anxiety each year. Finding a way of controlling this problem will not only reduce sickness and absenteeism costs; it will also have a positive effect on the following areas, all of which must be under control if a company is to be successful:

- Employees' commitment to work
- Staff performance and productivity
- Staff turnover
- Staff recruitment and retention
- Customer satisfaction
- Organisational image and reputation.

Home-workers will always state that not having to commute to work is one of the main benefits of working from home, as will be shown in greater detail in Chapter 10. The effect of eliminating this particular stressor becomes clearly visible when comparing the comparative output of home-based and office-based workers. Home-based workers start the day in a much more positive and therefore productive frame of mind, while office-based workers take some time to reach their optimum level of output.

Home-based workers are also able to work through minor ailments that will cause their work-based colleagues to take time off. For example, an office-based worker who wakes up in the morning with reoccurring bouts of diarrhoea is unlikely to travel into work. The thought of being caught short on the journey would deter even the most hardy of us. Usually this condition is only a minor ailment and within a few hours the symptoms will have

25

resolved themselves, but by this time the office-based worker will have phoned in sick and therefore take the rest of the day off. However, for the home-based employee this is not the case. As they have no journey into work they can work as normal, even if they do have to make a few more "toilet breaks".

The common cold is another classic example of where office-based workers loose out. A cold can make you feel lousy, but it doesn't actually stop you from working. Once again, the problem for the office-based worker is the thought of that journey in to work, having to stand on stuffy buses, tubes or trains. Even if the journey *is* undertaken, the problem for the office-based employee does not end there. Having made a superhuman effort to arrive at his desk, his work colleagues then complain like mad because they don't want to catch his cold. How often have you heard a manager say (with some reason): "Why didn't you stay at home? I don't want your cold spreading around the whole office." In this situation, no matter what he does, the office-based worker just can't win. However, for home-based workers things are totally different. They simply start work in the normal way, having taken a couple of tablets to help fight the effects of the cold. And because home-workers are less stressed, their immune system is far more effective at fighting the cold virus thereby reducing the severity.

The same reasoning can also apply for more serious situations such as broken limbs and infectious diseases.

Lower overhead costs

This is the second area where companies can make big savings by introducing home-working, for as sure as night follows day, reduced overhead costs will follow the implementation of home-based working. The reduced need for office space has obvious immediate benefits, and this flows through every level of overhead from rent and rates through to toilet rolls and vending machine supplies. There may even be a case for relocation of the head office to a less expensive area. This saving occurs because, by its very essence, home-based working eliminates the need to have large offices in easily accessible places, which usually means expensive town centres. Not only can companies reduce the size of their offices; they can also relocate to areas where the cost of office rent is greatly reduced.

Improved staff retention

Any company that employs a large numbers of salespeople will always suffer from high levels of staff turnover. And even with the latest recruitment developments on the net, replacing staff is still a costly, not to mention time-consuming business. New staff are also less productive during the first few months of their employment, because no matter how good they are there will always be a settling-in period. At present, home-based workers are far less likely to leave their jobs than their office-based colleagues. However, this anomaly will undoubtedly reduce as a larger number of companies take up the home-based working initiative, and a greater number of home-based jobs become available.

Reduced cost of commuting

The average worker in the UK commutes 2,906 miles a year and travels 1,622 miles on business by car. Commuting accounts for approximately 78.5 billion miles of car travel, with 44 billion miles driven while on business. With the above in mind it should come as no surprise that congestion on our over-used and outdated road system costs businesses billions of pounds. Although some of the more visible costs are borne by the employee, such as the cost of travel or petrol, which equates to an average of £500 per annum per employee, the invisible costs of inefficiency, missed appointments, and overrun schedules, also hit the employer. The cost of these congestion-related problems is estimated at £20 billion per annum, as good an incentive as any to introduce home-working and tele-conferencing.

A list of benefits received through implementing home-working can be seen in Fig 2:2 below:

Type of Saving	Home-working Benefits	Large Companies	Small Businesses
Major	Employment Costs	X	X
Major	Premises Costs	X	
Minor	Absenteeism	X	X
Minor	Staff Retention	X	X
Minor	Heating & Lighting	X	
Minor	Consumables	X	X

Fig 2:2 Home-working benefits for the employer

3

The Advantages of Home-Working for the Employee

If the home-working revolution is to gather pace and take its rightful position in the employment hierarchy then there have to be real benefits on offer for the employee as well as the employer. And the good news is that the employee comes out of this deal very nicely indeed. The benefits that are driving the home-working revolution from an employee's perspective are as follows.

Benefits for the employee

- No travelling time or costs
- Better work-life integration
- Reduction in work-related stress
- Healthier lifestyle
- Increased earning potential

No travelling time or costs

Oh, for the joy of commuting! Kicking your heels on a cold, wet platform as you search the horizon for the late running 7:42 to London. Then when it arrives, joy of joy, you have the pleasure of squashing yourself into an overcrowded carriage that seems to be full of a garlic-eating fraternity.

Even in the privacy of your own car you fare little better. The fiveways junction is grid locked as usual because the lights have failed once again. Having queued for fifteen minutes to get through the junction and on to the open road, yes you've guessed it, more traffic lights because the water company have dug up the road again. A slight exaggeration, maybe, but a recent survey of Europe's slowest roads doesn't offer much hope to the stressed out commuter. Yes, it's official; Britain has the slowest roads in Europe. In our worst affected City, London, traffic crawls along at an average speed of just 11.8mph, forty per cent slower than in Paris. In fact British Cities filled six of the ten slowest spots, with Manchester, Edinburgh, Glasgow, Bristol and Belfast also having average speeds under 20mph. So why are our roads so crowded? The survey claims it's all down to the under-investment in our public transport systems, which will come as no surprise to our harassed commuters.

Just when you thought it couldn't get any worse, we have the Underground system. A mobile sauna on wheels, with an atmosphere more dangerous to your health than the now defunct smokers' room. Trains crammed full of people, stuck in tunnels with no power, high temperatures that make it difficult to breathe, and not even enough room to faint. It's illegal to transport animals in such conditions, but apparently it's okay for us humans.

So, welcome to commuters' hell, where only a human would struggle so hard to get somewhere they really don't want to be. Surely there has to be a better way of getting our employees in front of their desks.

Okay, so I might have taken a slight liberty. The above doesn't happen every day – it just feels like it does. But joking aside, commuter stress is a debilitating experience, and one that definitely leads to reduced performance when you finally arrive at work. This trend is clearly visible when you compare the work pattern of a home-worker against that of an office-worker. (See Chapter 9.)

The second benefit of not having to commute to work is all that money you save. After a while, home-workers tend to take this benefit for granted, but it really does give you the extra finances to enjoy a better lifestyle, as can be seen in Fig 3:1 below. These extra finances can be used to fund a healthier life style, such as membership of a health club, or a few relaxing weekend breaks.

Average London Based Salary	Average London Commuting Cost	Annual Saving As Earned Income	Equivalent Pay Increase
25,000	1,800	2,520	10%

Fig 3:1 Saving of annual commuting costs

Not having to commute to work means the home-worker can live anywhere in the country, and if you are feeling really adventurous maybe even Europe. This benefit can be a real advantage for the home-worker as it means they no longer need to rent or buy a property within an expensive commuter belt. They could even cash in on an expensive London property and benefit from moving out to the less expensive suburbs, as can be seen in Fig 3:2.

Average Property Price	Average Property Price	Average Saving
London	332,009	-
South East	265,501	66,508
Yorks/Humber	164,601	167,408
East	229,466	102,543
South West	222,611	109,398
North west	163,032	168,977
East Midlands	172,558	159,451
North East	148,992	183,017
West Midlands	179,112	152,897

Fig 3:2 Average house prices

Better work-life integration

This is something you see mentioned in many training manuals but what is meant by a better work-life balance? The truth is that this will be different for each and every one of us, and will also vary at different times in our life such as when we are bringing up a young family. What this definitely doesn't mean is that our time is split 50-50 between work and home. Some people live to work – these are usually the high flyers, the great achievers – but the majority of us simply work to live, and our work-life balance will be dependant upon our lifestyle choice.

The high achievers will need to be at work in excess of 12 hours a day, and for them family life will always take second place. In order to clime the corporate ladder these employees will need to be seen achieving within the office environment, constantly around to take advantage of any opportunity that falls their way. Therefore, this type of employee will not be suited to a home-working role. However for the majority of us, those who work to live, home-working will offer a much better balance to their life. This balance is usually brought about through the elimination of the time and costs spent commuting to and from work. The time saved by not having to commute can then be spent socialising with friends and family. The financial savings made through not having to commute to work offer a greater spending power to the home-worker, and this extra money is usually spent on social activities such as joining health or sports clubs, developing hobbies such as photography, taking additional family holidays, or maybe visiting the theatre, to list just a few examples. All of these activities enhance your private life and will give you a better work-life balance.

Creating a better life for yourself can be taken even further, as happened with the first employee who trialled home-working for me. At the time of the trial, Amanda lived in London but has since relocated to Yorkshire. Amanda made a lifestyle decision, wanting to leave the hectic lifestyle of London and move back towards her roots. To her benefit, and ours, she was able to achieve this without having to leave her job. This is another example of how home-working can be a win/win scenario. Amanda achieved the better life style she wanted and the company managed to keep a very good employee.

Reduction in work-related stress

This theme will appear throughout the book, as it is part and parcel of home-based working, a benefit that is entwined in the very fabric of the process. Basically this reduction of stress will be brought about through the elimination of commuting stress, the elimination of office politics, and the ability to have greater control over your working environment. Stress will also be reduced by the healthier lifestyle associated with home-working.

Healthier lifestyle

This benefit is very much tied in with the reduction of stress as detailed above. The extra spending power that home-workers have is usually diverted into creating a healthier existence for themselves. Examples of this would be regularly attending health clubs, training to run marathons, increasing the number of hobbies undertaken.

Increased earning potential

Increased earning potential is usually achieved through two basic changes: firstly by eliminating the cost of commuting to work, and secondly by increasing earning potential through achieving better results on performance-related bonuses. Home-workers, like Amanda can also increase their level of free cash, by moving to areas of the country where housing and everyday subsistence costs are lower. Another way for home-workers to increase their earning potential is by utilising the extra personal time they gain through not having to commute, to turn hobbies, such as photography, into money-making ventures.

$$4$$

Other Advantages of Home-Working

Although it is the advantages gained by the employer and employee that are driving the growth of home-working, there are other advantages that we can all benefit from. I personally believe that these benefits are some of the most important to be gained from implementing home-working.

Our carbon footprint

The phrase "carbon footprint" is fast becoming one of the most overused phrases in the English language as the environment, and global warming in particular, looks set to become one of the major battlegrounds for the next parliamentary elections. But what are our politicians actually doing to improve things, to tackle what is probably one of the biggest challenges that mankind has faced in a generation? Making the occasional journey on a bicycle and putting a solar panel in the roof of your house may be good for the tabloid headlines, but it will do little to solve the problems we face today.

As the world has become more prosperous, and the average standard of living has increased, so the drain on our natural resources has ballooned out of control. For example, thirty years ago when I was a teenager the one car family was the norm; if you had two family cars you were rich. Today, as my own children approach a similar age, and definitely without being flush with money, I have two family cars and am rapidly moving towards a third as my youngest daughter has now started driving.

Another example of how things have changed can be seen from the number of televisions per household. Once again, when I was a teenager the norm was one television per household. Today I have four televisions in my home, which may sound excessive but is not uncommon if you have children. Whether we like it or not, life has changed. Whether it has changed for the better is mere conjecture, but the fact remains that it has changed and will continue to evolve with each new generation. What we need to do is find a way to adapt our lifestyle so that we don't end up destroying the world in which we live. I believe home-working has an important role to play in achieving this for the reasons stated below.

Reducing those greenhouse gases

This subject is a complex issue and one beyond the scope of this book. However, all experts would agree that greenhouse gases are starting to cause a substantial shift in global climate patterns, and that by far the biggest cause of this problem is the amount of Carbon Dioxide we pump into the atmosphere, mainly through power stations and vehicle emissions. If Governments are serious about tackling this issue they should offer companies tax breaks to promote home-based working. By encouraging people to work from home, commuter traffic could be reduced by forty per cent, while taking advantage of video-conferencing could reduce business trips by twenty per cent. This reduction in vehicle emissions far outweighs the savings made through congestion charging, which is more about raising revenue than improving the environment.

Home-working also reduces the need for companies to maintain large offices, which use copious amounts of energy to heat and light. I know home-workers will still need to light and heat their homes, but due to better insulation to prevent heat loss, and the reduction in the level of equipment required for the office in the home, there are still large savings to be made. Home-workers will also be more energy efficient when spending their own money; therefore they will put on a large woolly jumper rather than turn up the heating.

Reducing the drain on the NHS

Stress-related illness is a big drain on the resources of the National Health Service. Although home-working will not totally eliminate this problem, it will go a long way to reducing it, for reasons already explained (the reduction of commuter-based stresses and the development of healthier work-life balances).

The treatment of respiratory illnesses such as asthma is also an increasing burden on the health service, especially in large metropolitan cities where the continual increase has been linked to our reducing air quality. This is a trend that could be significantly reduced, if not reversed, by encouraging home-working with its associated benefit of reducing commuter traffic by forty per cent.

Regeneration of the local community

Home-based working will also help to rejuvenate local economies. The home-worker, as stated earlier in this book, will have an increased spending power, spending that will most likely take place within the local community. Home-workers will still need to eat and socialise during their lunch hours.

Reduced traffic flow

The reduction in commuter traffic would certainly reduce, and possibly eliminate altogether, the need to widen existing roads or build new ones. This would save great swaths of our countryside from being destroyed and preserve the natural habitat of our wildlife. Traffic would also flow more smoothly, hence being more fuel efficient, and therefore producing less harmful emissions.

5

Managing the Home-Worker

The popular perception of home-working has progressed over the last five years, with most people now accepting that it is feasible at least from a technical point of view. However, I guarantee that when you raise the issue in conversation, you will still get an overwhelmingly negative or cynical response – along the lines of: "You must be mad, they will be sitting at home doing nothing." Then you'll get all the jokes about cutting the grass, doing the ironing, or painting the walls. So, do they have a point? Is there any logic in what they say? No! No! No! As a manager would you allow the staff in your office fool around, let them sit there surfing the Internet all day? Of course you wouldn't, so why should it be any different for your home-working staff. Because you can't see what they are doing, I hear you all thinking. But that's the whole point – you can. I have a better understanding of what my home-workers are doing than those that work with me in the office, and that's because I have set up a managerial process for my home-workers that constantly feeds back that type of performance information. Just as a blind man has a brail book so that he can read, the manager of home-workers can use their computer and telephone to see into their office in the home.

At this point I think we should get one thing straight, if you have an office-based employee who is lazy and unreliable, then sending him to work from home will not change anything. He will still be lazy and unreliable. Home-working is not some kind of magic elixir that will turn a bad employee into a good one, and no-one has ever claimed that to be the case, but it will turn a good employee into an excellent one, a productive employee into a very productive employee.

So let us now look at the vital elements necessary to successfully manage a home-worker:

1. Ensure that all equipment is well maintained and working properly.
2. Make sure the home-worker has enough work to keep them busy.
3. Do not isolate the home-worker.
4. Make sure the home-worker has office- based support.
5. Don't forget to man manage the home-worker.
6. Set performance targets.

Well-maintained equipment

Regular maintenance of home-based equipment is an important part of supporting the home-worker. When equipment malfunctions in the office it may be annoying but there is usually something else you can do to keep yourself busy, or another computer you can use. If a home-worker's computer goes down they are literally cut off from the outside world. Without their umbilical cord to the office there is very little they can do. Proper maintenance of computer equipment is also important in order to maintain a reasonable operating speed, and to ensure as a company you meet current Health and Safety regulations.

Controlled workflow

Home-workers need to be kept busy. Otherwise, their minds can wander too easily. So getting their workload right is of great importance. This is not as easy as it sounds and a short period of trial and error may be necessary to achieve the right balance. In order to keep this trial period to a minimum it should be remembered that home-workers could be up to 100 per cent more productive than their office-based colleagues. When initially setting up a home-working process I would suggest setting a workload that is 60 per cent higher than that achieved in the office, and gradually working up from there.

No man is an island

No man, or a woman for that matter, is an island. We are all human. We all need social interaction, to belong, even home-workers. Therefore it is imperative that a structure is put in place to ensure that the home-worker continues to feel part of the company. This can be achieved by ensuring home-workers are included on all office emails and have access to the company intranet. My home-workers also attend the office at least once every two weeks, just to touch base and regroup. Home-workers will also talk to each other by phone, or send the odd joke by email, and before you start thinking differently, this is a good thing. A few minutes' light-hearted banter with their colleagues is one of the best ways to ease the feeling of isolation and make them feel part of the team.

Office-based support

Although home-workers need to be self-sufficient there will be some occasions when they will need support from workers in the office. This usually takes the form of supplying copies of documentation that they cannot access from home, although with the increased use of emails (and documents printed electronically to pdf files) this is a problem that will soon disappear. Any communication from home-based staff should always be dealt with as a matter of priority.

Out of sight, out of mind

It is all too easy to forget to manage the home-worker. Performance looks good, and targets are being reached, but are the wheels about to fall off? Being a good manager is all about communicating with your workforce, discussing problems, agreeing a strategy, and most important of all, praising good achievements. If you want to keep your home-workers motivated you need to let them know that you care about them, and that their achievements have not gone unnoticed. Working from home may offer the home-worker some good benefits, but like all benefits, over time they become the norm and can be taken for granted. Once that happens the honeymoon period will be over, and motivation and performance will once again be down to good personnel management.

Managing through performance targets

Performance targets are probably the most important factor of home-based working. Once set, they provide both the manager and the home-worker with instant feedback on performance. At a glance I can look at the data for my home-based credit controllers and know immediately how many chase calls an hour they are making, and how much money they are collecting. The home-workers will use the targets to plan their day, often setting themselves little goals like making three more chase calls before they make themselves a cup of tea. This may sound silly but these little sub targets really do allow the home-worker to power on and reach higher levels of productivity. However, one word of warning – when setting home-based performance targets, you need to get them right. While they need to push the employee, they still need to be achievable. If you work hard in the office but fail to reach your target because it was set to high, your manager can see the effort you put in and realise their mistake. The same is not true for home-workers, and their hard work can easily go unnoticed. If you continue to set home-based targets that are too high you will end up with very unmotivated staff, and you will not achieve the increase in productivity that you are looking for.

6

Developing a Home-Working System

Working from home is not simply a change in the working environment; it is a change in lifestyle. Like a magical elixir, home-working will increase productivity while reducing stress levels, increase profits for the company while increasing disposable income for the employee, increase an employee's leisure time and offer the company a healthier workforce. But all of this will only happen if we develop the correct home-working system. This system should take advantage of the latest developments in technology to help change our management style and the business support infrastructure. This system will need to be forward thinking and progressive, a system that fits nicely within a 21st-century business environment.

There is no doubt that in today's manic world companies have become a lot more demanding of their employees, especially those who occupy the middle and senior management positions. These increased demands play havoc with their work-life balance, dragging these important employees into a vicious circle of increased stress and falling productivity. This creates a destructive cycle that, if unchecked, will prevent any business from reaching its full potential.

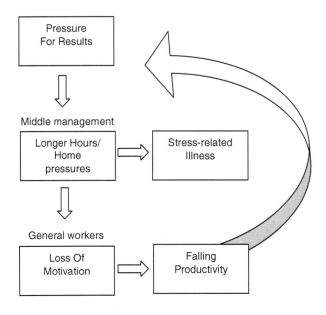

Insert fig 6:1 The pressure circle

If a home-working system is going to be successful it has to motivate the home-worker, and the best way to assess the effect of your home-working system on motivation is to look at the work of Abraham Maslow, a renowned psychologist, who more than sixty years ago identified five basic categories of personal motivation. Although Maslow stated a person would only be affected by one motive at any specific time, we need to know that our home-working system will support all five categories if it is to be successful.

Maslow's motivational categories

- Survival
- Safety and security
- A need to belong
- Self-esteem
- Self-development

If a Senior manager can find a way to satisfy these special needs within his managerial strategy he will have a happy, contented, and well-motivated workforce.

Survival

Survival is linked to having food to eat, water to drink, air to breath, and a roof over your head. Even if the home-worker sets up his office in a tent in his garden we would assume they could fulfil this basic need.

Safety and security

Many employees, especially those suffering from low self-esteem, are likely to be more susceptible to this motive. This type of motive is likely to be more prevalent during times of recession, when all employees feel less secure in their job, but it can cause problems for home-based workers at any time if they are not managed properly as this can lead to them feeling less secure in their role (see Chapter 10). This insecurity is likely to grow if the home-worker feels isolated because isolation leads to feelings of loneliness, and loneliness is a breeding ground for insecurity. On the positive side, as home-workers usually achieve better results then office-based staff they should feel more secure in their job and therefore less likely to job hop.

Need to belong

Maslow's thinking on this matter is that we all need a certain level of social interaction, a feeling that we belong. Although work partly fulfils this need, social interaction in our private life also plays a large part in satisfying this motive. This motive is one reason why home-workers can feel a little more isolated during stressful times in their personal lives. In order to cope with this type of motive, a home-working system needs to create an atmosphere where home-workers can still interact with each other, still feel they are an important member of the team. Home-working also offers more time for social interaction outside of work, which should also be of benefit.

Self esteem

An employee who is driven by this motive needs to know that they are valued as an individual, and home-based working is the ideal way to fulfil this need. This type of employee lives for the recognition that his actions are worthwhile, and home-based working, with its structure built upon the foundation of constantly monitoring performance, is the ideal way of fulfilling this need. This type of self-obsession can sometimes work against the success of the team, but if you create a strong team spirit the team itself can take on a single identity that this type of employee buys into; and then the success of the team becomes as important to him as his individual success.

Self-development

Maslow believed this was the highest form of human motivation, the desire to develop one's ability to the full. Home-working is heaven sent for employees who respond to this motive as it offers home-workers the following opportunities that will feed this motive:

- Working with cutting edge technology.

48

- The opportunity to control your own working environment.
- The chance to take responsibility for planning your own working day.
- The opportunity to achieve better results.
- The need to take more responsibility for your own performance.
- The opportunity to develop new skills.
- More personal time to develop private interests.

With the above in mind I see no reason why the home-worker should not be as motivated as the office-based worker. In fact, due to the better control over negative influences, and the opportunity for senior management to react immediately to the need for praising or reprimands, I believe the home-based worker will be even more motivated.

When developing a home-working system it is important to remember that home-working is a partnership between employer and employee. The system not only has to meet the requirements of the company but also the expectations of the employee. To recap from Chapters 2 and 3 the requirements of a home-based system are as follows:

The employer
- Increased productivity
- Reduced absenteeism levels
- Lower overhead costs
- Improved staff retention
- The cost of commuting

The employee
- No travelling time or costs
- Better work-life integration
- Reduction in work-related stress
- Healthier lifestyle
- Increased earning potential

A successful home-working system will need to satisfy all of the needs identified by Maslow and listed above, but the most important element of such a system is not actually included in this list. Home-based working is all about **trust**, and that's why many senior managers have trouble embracing the concept. Trust is something that is seriously lacking in many companies today, and it's that negativity that is the biggest threat to implementing a successful home-working system. If trust is to flourish two things need to happen. Firstly the Employer needs to feel confident with the monitoring processes he has built in to his home-based system. Secondly the employee will need to feel he is given responsibility for his own actions.

Invasion of the home-wreckers

Having developed a system that embraces all of the above, it is important to ensure that you don't wreck that system by allowing the office to take over the home. There is nothing worse than trying to relax with your loved one when all you can see out of the corner of your eye is the works computer, and a pile of work that needs to be done. When we leave the office at the end of the day, most of us switch out of work mode and re-enter our private persona, and home-based workers need to be able to do the same. Home-workers will find it difficult to switch off mentally at the end of the day if a constant reminder of work surrounds them.

Do not over-analyse

As previously stated, a home-based system, by necessity, will provide senior management with a plethora of performance-related information, but this information still needs to be used in the correct way. If senior management simply extract the negative results and react on these without giving any thought to the positive data, then the system will fail. It is also important to remember that the analysis should be measured over time. Nobody likes to feel they are continually being monitored, and one hour's poor performance in isolation tells you nothing. Home-workers are not super-human; just like office-based staff, they will also have an off day, so to get a true picture you need to judge their performance over a longer time-span. At Centaur, we measure performance over a rolling ten-day period, which works very well for us, although I accept that some companies may feel their process needs tighter control. There is nothing wrong with this. Each company needs to develop a system that suits their own needs, but I would not recommend going below a rolling 5-day period unless your staff are used to constant supervision. There is nothing to stop you accessing the data on an hourly basis if that is what you need to do to put your mind at rest, just don't judge a home-workers performance over too short a period.

A truly remarkable system

Up until now I have used the Centaur credit control system to explain the home-working process in this book. This is because our process is easy to measure and target, and therefore suites the home-working process. However, not all home-working processes fall into this category. We have recently introduced a home-working system for our "Accounts Payable" process that is totally different in its structure and implementation. Prior to implementing this new home-working process our office-based "Accounts Payable" team were seriously underperforming. Productivity was low, and team spirit was non-existent. Not what you would consider to be the ideal situation when thinking of introducing a home-based system. To make matters worse, unlike our credit control function, there was no easy way to target performance, and it certainly didn't seem to make sense to pay our "Accounts Payable" clerks a bonus for paying our suppliers more efficiently.

51

After much deliberation we decided not to offer our accounts payable clerks any form of bonus to drive up productivity but instead to play on their desire to work from home. After a long discussion we decided our goal was to reduce the length of time it took from the receipt of our suppliers invoice to the point where payment could be made. The main elements of this process were as follows.

- Scanning the invoice
- Indexing the invoice
- Chasing payment approval
- Uploading the invoices to our accounting system

The targets we set for our "Accounts Payable" team were quite simple: to clear all scanning, indexing, and uploading of invoices on a daily basis – which basically meant clearing all work by the end of the day. From day one, something very strange happened. Four individual workers suddenly started working together as a team. They supported each other, helped each other clear their workflows, and as a result productivity rose by approximately fifty per cent. Our "Accounts Payable" home-working process has now been running for six months and productivity levels are still edging upwards.

The success story of our "Accounts Payable" team proves that home-working can work, even for processes that are not as easily adaptable to this style of working. All you need are staff that truly want to work from home and a management that are willing to trust their staff. Achieve this, and all the benefits that go hand-in-hand with the home-working process will drive their performance forward. Once employees work from home they don't want to go back to working in an office and they will do anything to avoid that, even work harder and be more productive.

7

Measuring Performance

A company will never successfully implement home-working unless it first develops a proper system to measure performance – but not just any old system. To achieve the desired results the system must fulfil the employer's needs, but at the same time be one that home-worker can buy in to. An example of a system that would work for the manager, but not the home-worker, would be the installation of a webcam on the home-worker's computer, with a live link in to the office. While this option would definitely allow the manager to know exactly what the home-worker was doing, it would destroy any hope of that all-important trusting relationship, not to mention probably impinging on the employee's civil liberties.

Trust is an important part of any home-working relationship and there can be no trust if "Big Brother" is watching every move you make. So how do we get over the biggest misconception surrounding home-working: that the manager never knows what the home-worker is doing. And let's be honest, we can all understand this fear. After all, you would need to be one hell of a motivated worker to achieve your full potential when working from home with no supervision. The answer to this problem is quite simple and logical: the manager needs to design a system that not only measures performance, but also at the same time becomes the manager's eyes and ears. A well-designed home-working system will support the home-worker while at the same time offering the manager supervision by stealth.

As stated earlier in this book, each type of business will need to develop their own unique system, a system based around their own requirements and their own working practices. However, irrespective of what bell and whistles a company attaches to their system, they will always need to incorporate the same basic building blocks, which are as follows.

1. Define exactly what you are trying to achieve.

2. Isolate the definitive elements of the working process that will enable you to achieve your goal.

3. Set targets and measure performance on these definitive elements leading to increased productivity.

In order to explain this process I am going to discuss the successful system that I implemented for our Credit Control function, which has increased productivity by over 90 per cent.

Define what you are trying to achieve

When I first presented a home-working proposal to the company I work for I never dreamed that we would achieve such staggering increases in productivity. To be honest, if I had suggested increased productivity levels of 90 per cent I don't think anyone would have believed me. Initially we decided that we were looking to increase productivity by 50 per cent as the company was growing at a substantial rate and we were keen to cover this growth without the need to employ extra staff.

Isolate the definitive elements

As the main function of our Credit Control department is to collect money owed to the company by our customers, we targeted our increased productivity on the two elements that would enhance this process.

1. The number of effective chase calls made.
2. The number of sales queries resolved.

Setting targets to increase productivity

Our office-based credit controllers were achieving an average of 33 effective chase calls per day. Therefore we set our home-workers an initial target of making 50 effective chase calls per day, slightly above our required 50 per cent increase in productivity. All of our sales queries, which are resolved by the sales team, need to be chased on a weekly basis, so our home-workers simply needed to maintain this level of activity. Our credit controllers were already on a performance-based bonus that measured the total level of debt collected and the value of 90-day debt as a percentage of the ledger. As there is a direct link between the number of chase calls made and the amount of debt collected, our home-based controllers were able to increase the amount of bonus they earned, which in turn encouraged them to be even more productive.

Using the system to measure performance

So, now for the big question. How do I know my credit controllers are working hard at home and not sitting with their feet up watching daytime telly? Well, apart from the fact that only an insane person would actually want to watch daytime television, we actually log every collection call our credit controllers make through our telephone supplier's website. Then at the end of each day we print of a call report and analyse the data. The first procedure is to eliminate inter-company calls, and any external calls under 30 seconds in duration, which we do not consider to be effective calls. This leaves us with a list of effective calls showing their duration, the time the call was made, and the receiving telephone number. The receiving telephone number is not recorded in our results, but is a useful tool for spotting regular calls to friends or family. We then enter the call data into an Excel spreadsheet and create a ten-day call log, broken down into the seven working hours of the day, and from this data we can calculate an average ten-day call figure. For various reasons, call levels will fluctuate from day to day so we believe the average figure is the most accurate snapshot of how our credit controllers are performing.

	9:30-10:30	10:31-11:30	11:31-12:30	12:31-14:30	14:31-15:30	15:31-16:30	16:31-17:30	Total
Amanda Brown	6	9	9	14	10	7	10	65
	10	11	9	7	10	8	14	69
	10	11	9	10	6	8	9	63
	7	6	5	12	9	10	13	62
	9	7	10	9	10	13	11	69
	9	7	10	9	12	9	8	64
	10	11	7	11	6	8	5	58
	6	6	11	10	7	9	11	60
	10	9	10	10	9	10	7	65
Avg Calls Per Hour	11	7	8	12	7	6	16	67
	9	8	9	10	9	9	10	64

	9:30-10:30	10:31-11:30	11:31-12:30	12:31-14:30	14:31-15:30	15:31-16:30	16:31-17:30	Total
Mine Isaac	7	5	10	9	6	3	0	40
	11	3	13	20	26	4	0	77
	15	0	11	7	12	16	4	65
	10	13	6	11	20	13	3	76
	4	6	11	16	15	6	6	64
	2	14	2	12	5	20	6	61
	6	12	13	21	8	20	9	89
	6	14	20	20	17	13	9	99
	5	4	0	23	16	6	1	55
Avg Calls Per Hour	13	3	6	6	7	2	0	37
	8	7	9	15	13	10	4	66

	9:30-10:30	10:31-11:30	11:31-12:30	12:31-14:30	14:31-15:30	15:31-16:30	16:31-17:30	Total
Michael Preville	13	7	10	4	8	12	6	60
	8	3	8	2	7	5	4	37
	6	12	14	7	12	10	10	71
	6	5	13	7	11	12	7	61
	11	11	8	4	13	2	3	52
	8	9	10	2	8	11	2	50
	14	6	7	7	9	10	7	60
	14	8	9	6	11	12	8	68
	9	12	12	0	13	6	8	60
Avg Calls Per Hour	9	8	8	4	9	12	6	56
	10	8	10	4	10	9	6	58

Fig 7:1 Credit controllers' call activity log

From the call activity log we produce two graphs that help us to monitor and motivate our credit controllers. The first of these is the "Call Activity" graph, which allows us to measure an individual controller's performance against other home-based workers.

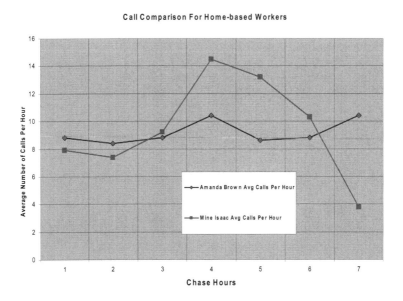

Call Comparison For Home-based Workers

Fig 7:2 Call activity graph

As can be seen from the activity graph above, our credit controllers can achieve comparable total call figures, yet have totally different working patterns. Amanda is a very steady consistent worker, who deals with her admin as and when it arises. This graph also mirrors Amanda's personality, which in itself is very calm, reliable and tidy. Mine on the other hand is a far more volatile personality with peeks and troughs of emotion, so it is not surprising to see this reflected in her call activity. However, on closer examination of Mine's results, I am sure you all want to know what she does between 4:30 and 5:30, when her call level drops of alarmingly.

Don't worry it's nothing sinister. She simply deals with her admin work during the last hour of the day, unlike Amanda who deals with her admin as and when it arises. This type of analysis allows us to understand the working pattern and performance of our home-based workers much more effectively than that of our office-based workers, as minute-by-minute analysis of office-based performance is impossible.

The second graph we use is the "Average Call Comparison" graph, which plots the average call results of each credit controller on the same graph. This is a great way of creating competition between the credit controllers and motivating them to produce even better results. This information is emailed to the credit controllers each morning with lavish praise for those at the top of the performance rating.

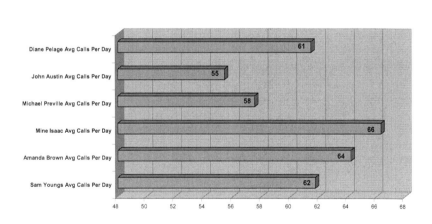

Fig 7:3 Average daily call comparison

59

Purely as a management tool we also plot the number of calls made by our home-workers against those made by office-based staff, to ensure that performance levels are not dropping. This graph highlights the benefits received through home-working, as will be discussed in greater detail in the next chapter.

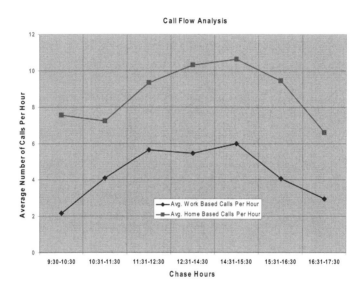

Fig 7:4 Working type comparisons

8

Evaluating the Successful Results

Our latest figures show that the increase in productivity of our home-based credit controllers has now peaked at over 100 per cent. Without any other changes to systems, staff, or procedures, the number of chase calls has increased from an average office-based level of 30 calls per day, to an average home-based level of 61 calls per day. This increase has enabled us to downsize the department through natural wastage, while at the same time absorbing high levels of growth brought about through company acquisitions.

Home-working is a senior manager's dream, an offer too good to refuse, that really does do what it says on the tin. Home-working offers management the best opportunity to reduce overhead and staffing costs, while at the same time massively increasing productivity. So why does this simple concept work so well?

The **four steps** to success and increased productivity are

1. Increased working hours.
2. The setting of clear goals.
3. Creating a competitive edge.
4. Creating a good team spirit.

Increased working hours

When I speak to the uninitiated about home-working, their first reaction is always to assume the home-worker will do less work, but nothing is further from the truth. Home-workers actually work longer hours because they exploit what used to be their travelling time to help them reach their targets. At the beginning of the day they will utilise their travelling time to set up their working environment, and at the end of the day they will utilise their travelling time to finish off those time-consuming admin tasks. By using this additional time our credit controllers can concentrate during the day on their primary task, which is making chase calls and generating cash flow.

As stated earlier in this book, commuting to work is a stressful business, with the office-based worker often arriving at work in an exhausted state. Because of this anomaly the office-based employee is never going to be as productive as the stress-free home-worker during the first hour of the day. This effect can clearly be seen in the graph comparing home-based and office-based call rates shown at the end of the previous chapter – reproduce below as Fig 8:1:

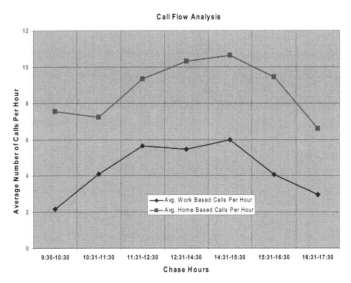

Fig 8:1 Working type comparisons

As can be seen in Fig 8:1 the two data lines on the graph follow a very similar path, but the home-worker starts the day at a much higher call level. The reasons for this are firstly because they are starting the day in a stress-free state, and secondly they also start work as soon as they sit at their desk. This is not the case with office-based workers who will probably spend the first fifteen minutes of the day using the toilet after their journey to work, getting a cup of coffee from the vending machine, and having a chat with colleagues about last night's football, or the latest soap storyline. There is a lot of time wasted before the office-based worker finally settles down to work.

The remainder of the graph in Fig: 8:1 shows how home-workers consistently make more calls an hour than their office-based colleagues. The reason for this increased call level is that home-workers are not distracted in the same way as their office-based colleagues. Unless our home-workers are going mad there is nobody to talk to, so it is easier for them to get into a groove and churn out those all important chase calls. The fact that home-based workers can control their own environment also helps to increase their productivity. A prime example of this can be found with employees who smoke. Office-based workers who smoke will waste at lease thirty minutes a day on cigarette breaks, while home-workers can smoke to their heart's content without having to leave their desk, and more importantly their phone. You will also find office-based workers complaining that the office is too hot, or too cold, whereas the home-based worker can set an ambient temperature that suits them.

The setting of clear goals

Home-based working can be very successful but it can also be a complete disaster, and there is usually a very fine line between the two outcomes. You cannot take an office-based worker and drop them in front of a computer at home without any thought about managing them remotely, and expect everything to work out fine.

Home-workers need a supportive system tailored to their needs, as discussed in Chapter 7, but they also need clear goals so that they know what they are aiming for, and clear feedback so that they know how well they are achieving. Management may set global targets, but it is the small individual goals that home-workers set themselves which make home-working so successful. These personal goals cannot be set with any kind of accuracy, unless home-workers are aware of what is expected of them.

The most important element of home-working is to make sure the home-worker is kept busy. There is nothing more demoralising for a home-worker than scratching around looking for something to do. Therefore, the first thing a manager needs to do is to make sure that working levels are set as accurately as possible. This may require some initial tinkering with targets, which the home-worker should be informed of from the start. This tinkering usually results in raising the workload over the first month or two, as it is more common for the manager to underestimate what can be achieved by the home-worker.

As I stated earlier, each home-working system will be tailored to your own company's needs, therefore the way you target your home-workers will also be unique. However, if I use our credit controllers as an example once again, this will hopefully give you an understanding of how the process can work in practice. When we initially set up our home-working process we set three specific goals that had to be reached if we were to continue with the trial. At this stage I should point out that you don't need a long list. Refine the working process to three or four main elements and concentrate your targeting on these. The required level of performance for our credit controllers was set as follows.

1. The need to make at least 50 effective chase calls a day (calls longer than thirty seconds in duration).

2. The need to chase, at least weekly, any outstanding queries with our sales teams.

3. The need to maintain the same levels of collection. (It was not our aim to necessarily collect more money by using home-workers, but to collect the money more cost efficiently. In actual fact we achieved both.)

The most important element for us, the root process from which everything else could grow, was the number of chase calls our home-workers made. Therefore, to ensure the success of our home-working trial, we knew that we needed absolute control over this element.

As explained in the previous chapter, we calculate the level of chase calls per day by taking an average over a ten-day period. Even with home-workers there will be good days and bad days so this seemed the fairest way of measuring this important process. Although we measure this performance as an average over a rolling ten days, we still look at each day's results to pick up on any problems or worrying trends. As we saw in Chapter 7, this data is then represented in a graph showing comparative daily call rates of each home-based worker. This was shown in Fig 7:3 and is reproduced again below in Fig 8:2.

Average Number of Home-based Calls

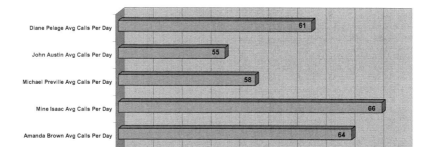

Fig 8:2 Comparison of home-based workers daily call rates

If there are any problems with our home-based workers; the level of calls they make or the timing of their calls, this will become very clear when we analyse their call data, as can be seen in Fig 8:3.

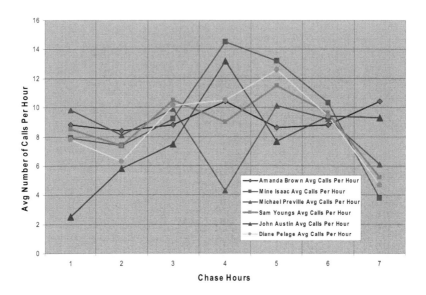

Fig 8:3 Hourly call comparisons for home-based workers

The graph in Fig 8:3 clearly shows that Michael Preville's call level falls alarmingly during the 4th hour, which represents the half hour before the lunch break and the half hour after the lunch break. By looking at these figures it could be assumed that Michael is extending his lunch hour. However, when we questioned him on his results it transpired that he uses the half hour before lunch to clear some of his admin work, which means no calls are made during this period and therefore the call level drops.

If we look at the results for Diane Pelage we can see that her calls fall away during the last hour of the day. Once again this could be representative of an employee who is finishing work early. However, as with Michael, Diane uses the last half hour of the day to deal with her admin, which means no calls are made during this period.

Our credit controllers also have access to the graph shown in Fig 8:2, comparing all home-workers' average daily call rates, so that they can measure their performance against that of their colleagues.

The comparison of home-workers' daily call rates is also a useful tool for managers to monitor the performance of individual credit controllers.

As previously stated, although we measure results as a ten-day average we still monitor the credit controllers results on a daily basis, as it is this data that is going to give us an early warning of any problems that may be emerging. One bad day's results means nothing, but if a poor trend is appearing over three or four days then it is worth a call to the home-worker just to make sure everything is okay.

This type of analysis is also an ideal way to highlight any home-worker who is taking liberties with the hours they work, those people who think that home-working is about having an easy time of it. The results for this type of worker are likely to look something like those shown in Fig 8:4 below.

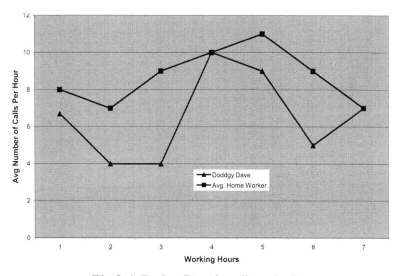

Fig 8:4 Dodgy Dave's call analysis

As can be seen, the reduced call levels in the graph clearly show where Dodgy Dave is putting his feet up. Measuring Dodgy Dave's results against the average results for all home-workers shows where you would normally expect the performance graph to rise and fall.

Creating a competitive edge

A little good-hearted competition works wonders to help maintain productivity, and there is no reason why this competitiveness cannot work for home-workers. Every day our credit controllers receive feedback on their performance, and part of that feedback is the comparative daily call rate graph referred to above (shown in Fig 7:3 and Fig 8:2).

Although each credit controller is set the same initial target, to make at least 50 effective chase calls a day, there is still a desire amongst the team to make more calls than their colleagues. We all want to be the best, and there's no reason why we can't be; it only takes a little time and effort. To help encourage this competitive edge, we analyse each credit controller's performance on a monthly basis and award a performance score, which accumulates over six months. Then twice a year we get together for a meal and give awards to the top three performers.

As referred to in earlier sections, the comparative daily call rates are calculated on the basis of a ten-day rolling average. By measuring the credit controllers' performance in this way, one good or bad day will not distort the figures; therefore any improvement in performance can only be achieved through a concerted effort over time.

Creating a good team spirit

It seems to me that there have been more management books written on team spirit than any other: how to achieve team spirit, how to apply team spirit to achieve your goals, the psychology of team spirit, and so on. What you won't find is a book entitled *Team Spirit for Home-Workers.* And why won't you find it? Because none of these management gurus believe it is possible. It flies in the face of the logic they preach which is as follows: "You can't have remote workers working together as a team; team spirit is created through face-to-face contact, not through emails and the telephone." All I have to say in reply is that this is simply not true – as evidenced by the fact that my home-workers display excellent team spirit.

I have always believed that team spirit is created when people have a common goal, a common foe to fight against. And I don't really believe that it matters whether that foe is a group of debtors who are reluctant to pay their bills, or some type of adversity that brings the group together. An example of this adversity is where a football team seems to play with much more spirit and determination after one of their team has been sent off.

I think there is a stigma that surrounds home-working, a belief that it is not really a proper job, and I think that fighting against this stigma can draw a home-working team together. Home-working can also be a lonely existence at times, something that most home-workers will experience, usually during times when there are problems in their private lives. At times like this the other home-workers will empathise with them and band together to carry the extra workload and help their colleague out.

Home-workers are more productive than their office-based colleagues – that's a fact – and they take pride from that and work hard to maintain that status. Once again, this status binds the home-workers together, and drives them forward to achieve even better performances.

Sometimes individual personalities can destabilise an office-based team, causing disharmony and creating a difficult working atmosphere. This disharmony is usually caused by very ambitious employees whose only concern is climbing the corporate ladder. Home-workers, by the very fact of their isolation, do not suffer from this problem. Personalities that may not jell in a normal office environment, can work quite happily as part of a home-based team, even those who are very ambitious.

9

The Whole Truth and Nothing *But* the Truth

It is very easy for me to sit here and sell you the benefits of home-working, for I believe passionately in the benefits it brings. But, as we all know, just because someone is passionate about something it doesn't necessarily make it right. Are home-workers *really* more productive? Do they *really* like working from home? Does the company *really* benefit from using a home-based team? While I can easily verify the performance data I have used in this book, it's not so easy to verify the feelings of our home-workers, so I thought I would let them talk to you direct, so that you could get the truth from the horse's mouth, so to speak.

Mine

Mine is in her thirties and lives with her partner in a house in north London.

I formed part of the second trial phase of home-working at Centaur, so I had already seen first-hand the benefits it could bring, although initially I wasn't sure it was going to be right for me. However, the thought of no more travelling to work and the opportunity to earn more money through increased productivity convinced me to give it a go. Now, five years later, I wouldn't dream of working any other way.

The benefits of home-working are far more varied than I originally thought they would be. As well as avoiding the stress of travelling on the tube every day, I found I was able to get so much more work done at home. By working from home I am also shielded from any office politics, which I could never abide. However, one word of warning, don't be surprised if you put on a little weight as Home-working increases the temptation to nibble snacks.

At times you can feel a little detached from the office, especially during times of change, such as the appointment of a new Departmental manager, or the acquisition of new companies, which can affect your own working structure. You can also feel very isolated in times of severe personal strife, but chatting to colleagues can help.

If my present company decided to stop home-working I would definitely try to find another home-working role. At home, to a certain extent, you are your own boss and I would definitely miss that. I would also miss the trust that management place in their home-workers. At some stage in the future I plan to have a family, and I believe home-working is more flexible and therefore can work in tandem with the pressures of bringing up a young family.

Michael

Michael is in his forties. He has two teenage children and resides in a house in Kent.

I used to have a long journey into work everyday and this factor alone persuaded me to take up the offer to trial home-working. I have two very active teenagers who place high demands on my time, and in this respect home-working has been a godsend. I have become accustomed to the increased leisure time that home-working offers, and would definitely miss this if I had to return to working in an office. Because I had a long journey in to work I would often arrive feeling exhausted – not the best way to start the working day. But now I am fully refreshed when I start work and this sets a good trend for the rest of the day. In my lunch hour I tend to walk through the woodland park opposite my house, which is far more rejuvenating than sitting at an office desk eating overpriced sandwiches, which I had to queue up for twenty minutes to buy.

Even when working from home you can still have bad days, especially during times of personal stress, and during these times you can feel a little isolated. However, you can still pick up the phone and talk to a colleague, and this does help. You can feel a little less secure as a home-worker, especially during times of redundancy, and the continual monitoring of your performance could be annoying if it was abused.

I live in a small village in the middle of nowhere and at times this can increase the feelings of isolation, however, I still talk to my colleagues on a regular basis and this helps to reinforce the feeling of team spirit. Providing all our systems are working correctly, and my performance is going well, then I don't really have time to feel isolated. The working day certainly seems to pass a lot quicker when working from home and I like that. If for any reason I lost my home-working job I would definitely try to find another. Obviously I need to work so would take an office-based job, but I think I would find it hard to acclimatise to this type of working environment. I would miss the freedom that comes with home-working and the opportunity to manage my own working day.

73

Sam

Sam is in her thirties and lives with her partner in a house in London.

I was one of the last credit controllers to work from home, as for a long time I didn't feel it was right for me. However, I am driven by money, and working from home was certainly enabling the other credit controllers to earn more, so I decided to give it a go. I was surprised how quickly I did adapt to home-working. I became a lot more productive which increased my job satisfaction. I have always taken pride in my work, and home-working enables me to achieve more, which gives me a lot of satisfaction. I also enjoy the increased leisure time that home-working offers, and I now go swimming before work most mornings. I also feel a lot less stressed since I have worked from home, not only in my work life but also in my private life.

I lived quite close to work, so travelling was not such a problem for me, although I still appreciate not commuting as a benefit of home-working. But for me the main benefits are reduced stress levels and not getting sucked into office politics. Home-working has allowed me to feel a lot more contented in my job, which, given the time we have to spend working, can only be a good thing.

I do feel isolated at times, as all home-workers do, but I find chocolate biscuits help, as well as a quick chat with one of my other home-working colleagues. There is no doubt that the feelings of isolation can be worse during the winter months or when you have problems in your private life. I have always been worried about job security and working from home has not altered this feeling in any way.

If for some reason I should lose my current job I would definitely look for another home-based role. I find the freedom of working on my own initiative so invigorating; I like having that control over my working life. So after four years do I regret working from home, not in the slightest. In fact I would try to keep my present job even if I moved abroad. Home-working has no location boundaries so why not live in one country and effectively work in another. Home-working offers freedom on so many levels.

74

Diane

Diane is in her forties, married, and lives with her husband and teenage children in a house in Kent.

All of Centaur's credit control staff had worked in the London office for some years before they transferred to home-working, but I was the first credit controller they employed to work immediately from home. I was attracted to the job because it offered me what I consider to be the ideal working experience. Working from home allows me to work with fewer distractions, be more productive and achieve better results. By working from home I feel as if I am my own boss. I like taking responsibility for my own actions. By working from home I am also financially better off and can help to provide a better standard of living for my family.

Although I feel very much part of the credit control team and enjoy meeting up with my work colleagues or talking to them on the phone, I do not miss working in an office environment. Unlike some of my other colleagues I never feel isolated when I work from home. I feel very secure in my job and cannot imagine working back in an office. One day I would like to move closer to my family who live in the West Country, and home-based working would allow me to do this without having to give up my job. Quality of life is very important to me and home-working offers the perfect work-life balance.

Amanda

Amanda is in her early thirties and lives with her partner in a house near the Yorkshire Dales.

I was the first person at Centaur to work from home and the two things that appealed to me when I was asked to trial the process were the elimination of commuting to work, and the potential increase in leisure time. I was training for my first London marathon at the time, so the increase in leisure time helped immensely.

Home-working offers so many benefits but not all of them are obvious when you first consider working from home. I think all home-workers would list not needing to travel to work and the resulting reduction in subsistence costs, along with increased leisure time, as their main benefits. However, once you work from home you realise these are not the only benefits. I worked in the West End of London and found it impossible to resist the shops in Oxford Street, which I visited regularly during my lunch hour. Working from home has definitely reduced my expenditure on items of clothing that I really didn't need – money that I now use to improve my quality of life.

For me the greatest benefit to arise from home-working has been the chance to move closer to my family. Although I hail from Scotland I had lived in London for a number of years with my partner, who originally came from Yorkshire. About two years ago we decided that we wanted to move away from London in search of a better quality of life. I was also keen to move closer to my parents who still live in Scotland. Trying to find a job in the Yorkshire area would have been difficult enough, but finding a job that paid London wages would have been impossible. Luckily for me, home-based working means you are not restricted to local commuter areas, with their inflated house prices. So home-working has given me the opportunity of a life time, an affordable house, located in a beautiful part of the country, with a gentler pace of life.

76

On the downside home-working can leave you feeling a little isolated at times, and I wouldn't recommend it to someone who lived on their own. On occasions you can also feel a little less secure in your job, especially if there are big changes going on within the company. However, the benefits far outweigh the negative aspects and out of choice I would never go back to working in an office again.

Paul

Paul is in his late thirties and lives with his wife and two young children in a house in Kent.

I was the last member of Centaur's credit control team to leave the office and work from home. The dynamics of the office had changed as more and more of my colleagues chose to work from home, and it was this change that finally led me to consider home-working.

Now three years later I have a much better understanding of the benefits home-working offers me. Apart from the usual benefits that I am sure my colleagues have already mentioned, home-working has offered me one special benefit, and that is more time to spend with my family. I have two very young children – in fact my second child has only just been born – and the increased leisure time that home-working offers has allowed me to play a much greater role in their life.

Apart from a better quality of life Home-working also offers a number of cost saving benefits that have increased my level of disposable income, income I can use to offer my family a better standard of living. There are drawbacks to home-working, mainly the fact that you can feel isolated at times, but the benefits definitely make it worthwhile. However, if you are considering working from home it helps if you have a room to use as an office that shuts you away from the rest of the house. This is definitely an advantage if you have two young children running around the house all day.

I have never worried about job security and working from home has definitely not changed this. Providing I produce the desired results I am sure that my position is no less secure than it would be working in the office. I would definitely recommend home-working to anyone, apart from anything else it is nice to feel as if you are your own boss. I found that an office could sometimes be a negative place, and I certainly don't miss the office politics that exist in every conventional office.

The manager's perspective

Home-based working is not only about changing the working process for the home-worker. The manager also has to accept change and learn to adapt. Managing home-workers is not simply a case of transferring normal office procedures into the home, as home-based working needs a far more sophisticated flow of information between the Employee and the manager.

One of the biggest changes for the manager is that he will no longer be able to control a workers performance purely by his presence, or body language, and will therefore need to work on better ways of communication. The phone and email will be the primary form of communication, although video-conferencing is another good option if your budget stretches to it. I personally decided against video-conferencing because I felt that putting a camera into our workers' homes was an intrusion too far. I believe that this is technology that could easily be abused and offers little in real benefit, but that is simply my personal view. If you do go for this option I believe that it should be the home-worker's decision as to when the conferencing facility is made available.

79

Kevin's story

Kevin is the manager of our accounting services and has managerial responsibility for three of our home-workers.

As a manager of home-workers it is not easy for me to know exactly what my staff are doing every minute of the day, so one of the things I needed to learn was not to micro-manage my home-workers. This was something easier said than done, as I used to have a very hands-on style of management.

I make sure that I speak to my staff at least once every day so that they know I am interested in what they are doing. The worst thing a manager can do is to rely solely on performance data to make decisions and forget to manage the human element. As we have seen from the home-workers comments listed above, home-working can sometimes lead to a feeling of isolation, and poor man-management techniques will increase this feeling. As I have gained greater experience managing home-workers, I have learnt to adapt my management style to minimise this problem.

As the manager of home-based staff I believe that it is important to catch my staff doing something right and to praise them for it. As a home-worker, it is easy to wonder if all your hard work is going un-noticed back in the office, and the simple recognition of your efforts by your manager can quickly disperse this feeling.

I find that home-based staff are far more willing to work on their own initiative once they leave the office, which enables me to take a step back and manage from a distance. This remote management style allows me more time to concentrate on the other elements of my job.

Conclusions

Having read the accounts above it becomes clear that home-workers do suffer feelings of isolation at times, especially during periods of personal upheaval. However, the feelings of isolation are not severe enough to compromise the home-working process, as every home-worker stated that they are committed to home-working. And there certainly does not seem to be any feeling that home-working destroys team spirit, which is one of the negative claims levied against it by the uninitiated.

What does become clear is that while financial rewards may initially be the most appealing factor, it is the feeling of being in control of their own destiny, and the increased amount of leisure time that persist over the longer period. This should not surprise anyone, as we all know that pay increases are only motivational for a very short period of time. We quickly get used to having, and spending, that extra money.

Surprisingly, for me anyway, home-working does seem to increase negative feelings on job security, and this is definitely something I need to look at further, because it shouldn't. From the statements above, I would suggest that companies should make more effort in talking to home-workers when changes are going on in the office. Ignoring how these changes may impact on the home-workers' feeling of security is unforgivable, and one that must be addressed. However, I take much satisfaction from the undeniable truth that all home-workers believed home-working was a more rewarding and productive way of working – and a process they definitely didn't want to change. Companies should also take heart from the fact that all home-workers stated that working from home made it less likely that they would look for another job. This is a big bonus for companies as they can retain experienced staff, eliminating that annoying reduction in productivity that is inevitably linked to the training of new personnel, and at the same time reduce their recruitment costs.

Revisiting the Obsolete Office Survey

As part of my first home-working book, *The Obsolete Office*, I carried out a survey to establish people's views on the benefits and disadvantages of home-working. Now that I have implemented and managed a home-working process for five years, I thought it would be interesting to see how accurate people's perceptions are when it comes to home-working.

Rating the benefits

The original survey came up with the following results when people were asked to rate the benefits of home-working.

- No need to commute   19%
- Flexible working   18%
- Reduced stress   17%
- Increased leisure time   16%
- Reduced subsistence costs   15%
- Environmental improvement   15%

Despite everything that has been written about our carbon footprint my home-workers still don't seem to consider the benefit to the environment when looking at the benefits of home-working. Flexible working definitely comes into the equation for our part time staff, although not for our credit controllers. The rest of the benefits were spot on.

Rating the disadvantages

The original survey came up with the following results when people were asked to rate the disadvantages of home-working.

- Lack of social interaction   22%
- Loss of team spirit   20%
- Distraction of working in the home   17%
- Working to targets   15%
- Working on own initiative   14%
- Too much leisure time   12%

Deciding on the disadvantages obviously proved a lot more difficult as the results were way off the mark. Once people start to work from home the perceived disadvantages just don't materialise. Apart from the lack of social interaction, all of the other disadvantages contained in the original survey are now considered to be advantages or non-existent by my home-based team.

Improved working conditions

The original survey asked office-based employees how their present working conditions could be improved and they replied as follows

- Flexible working   24%
- Improved environment   21%
- Less travel time/cost   20%
- Improved technology   14%

Working from home fulfils all of the above desires and that is why once employees work from home they don't want to return to an office-based job.

11

The British Telecom Survey

So far in this book we have focused largely at my implementation of a home-based working system at Centaur, but home-working is also being adopted by other, much larger organisations, and as stated earlier, the scaleable benefits offered by home-working can be really attractive to these larger companies. Large organisations such as British Telecom can see an increase in profits by implementing home-based working, and as a by-product they will also improve their green credentials by offering substantial benefits to the environment.

The British Telecom system

British Telecom has implemented a large-scale home-based working project called "Workabout", and BT claim this has enabled it and its staff to be more agile and efficient. BT Implemented "Workabout" to reduce the cost of running their estate and to better support the many differing work styles they have in operation.

SustainIT and Bradford University conducted two new surveys of BT employees in 2006, entitled *E-working at BT*, and *Conferencing at BT*. The idea of the surveys was to enable BT to understand the economic, social and environmental impacts of "Workabout", and the services that support it.

Some salient points from these surveys are now listed below.

E-Working at BT

BT has over 13,000 home-based employees who work at home an average 2.1 days per week. Surprisingly, 88 per cent of these workers are managers. These home-workers use a variety of connection portals to stay in contact with their office. The most popular form of connection to their office is via a broadband line (88 per cent). Wireless connections outside of the home are used by 33 per cent, while 17 per cent have a mobile email handset. Another surprising statistic is that 84 per cent of BT home-workers use telephone and video -conferencing services.

Home-based working helps employees to maintain a good work-life balance

30 per cent of BT's home-based workers stated that working from home had reduced domestic tension, while a further 37 per cent believe it would now be impossible, or at least very difficult, to do their job if they couldn't work from home. BT's workers save on average 4.4 hours a week by not commuting to work. And last but not least, a staggering 78 per cent make use of local services such as shops and sports facilities.

On the negative side, 46 per cent of home-based workers felt more isolated from their work colleagues than they did two years ago. However, isolation seems to be a growing trend across all working sectors as 37 per cent of office-based staff also felt more isolated.

Good for the environment

BT have no doubt that home-based working has genuine environmental benefits. They believe that travel-related CO_2 emissions have reduced by 3,663 tonnes per year, which equates to 13 per cent of the total company car fleet emissions.

54 per cent of home-based workers also believe they have printed less material over the last two years. This equates

favourably with the total workforce figure of 37 per cent, and has a positive benefit on the environment.

Conferencing at BT

The survey of employees who use telephone and video-conferencing showed these services have both personal and business benefits. The major benefits obtained through conferencing are listed below:

- 67 per cent of conference calls had definitely or probably replaced a face-to-face meeting

- 53 per cent believed this had saved them at least 3 hours of travelling per call as a result.

- A further 68 per cent of employees believed that conferencing has improved their work performance.

- 54 per cent of employees believe that conferencing has improved their work-life balance.

Extending the survey results to BT as a whole, conferencing eliminates 338,607 face-to-face meetings each year and significantly reduces business travel.

BT believes there is also a benefit to the environment for the following reasons.

- Each call prevented an average 288 miles of travel.

- 42 per cent of avoided journeys would have been by car, and 79 per cent of these would have been made during peak travel times. These figures suggest that conferencing helps relieve traffic congestion and pressure on public transport.

- The use of conferencing at BT has saved at least 54,000 tonnes of travel related CO_2 emissions per year.

- Conferencing has also saved BT £81 million of travel and subsistence costs, and frees up £54 million of management time. BT estimate that these cost benefits are 10-15 times greater than the cost of conferencing services.

12

The Greater Perspective

Do you ever read the papers and wonder if the world is going mad, or is it just me? In the last few weeks I have seen a number of scary headlines based on the premise of improving the commute to work – proposals that range from the downright costly to the downright dangerous. So why don't our politicians open their eyes and look at encouraging the most simplistic and cost-effective proposal to ease our commuting and congestion nightmare?

If the Government of this country were to offer tax breaks to companies who promote home-based working, this would substantially increase the take-up rate, and mean that we could make serious and immediate inroads into the following problems:

- Overcrowding on our roads.
- Meeting our Co2 Emissions.
- Relieving commuter stress.
- Reducing the ever-increasing burden on the NHS.

Research carried out for the European Community suggests that there are upward of 60 million jobs across Europe that could be converted to a home-working role. And a further survey carried out by the RAC states that if all the people who could work from home in the UK took up that option, we could reduce commuter traffic by 45 per cent. And we could improve matters even further if we used the option of video- and tele-conferencing rather than taking business trips.

Crossrail

Crossrail is a sixteen billion pound project designed to help improve the strain on our overcrowded transport system – a system designed to help cope with the projected increase in commuter traffic over the next two decades. Now for the bad news: Crossrail is not predicted for completion until 2017, which means I doubt if we will see it until well into the 2020s. We could have had three new governments in that time, with numerous spending reviews, and at least two recessionary cycles, so there is no guarantee that we will ever see fulfilment in its current form. And even if we do, going on past history, it is likely to cost far more than the original estimate of £16 billion. The idea of Crossrail, after all, has been around for many years, with just as many promises that never transpired.

After completion, Crossrail is expected to cater for 40 per cent of the extra rail capacity London will need by 2015, according to the official statements made by Crossrail. So I have two questions to ask about the development of this system:

1. What do we do about the extra rail capacity required until Crossrail comes on line? Crossrail's own information states that we will need this extra capacity by 2015, but Crossrail will not be complete until 2017.

2. Even when Crossrail is fully operational it will only service 40 per cent of the expected increase in rail travel, so how do we cope with the additional 60 per cent of the increase? How do we absorb this into an already overstretched rail system? For me the answer is simple: we can't, unless we find other alternatives to help.

By offering tax breaks to companies to encourage them to introduce home-working, the Government could decrease total commuter traffic by up to 45 per cent within the same time frame. And what's more the improvement could start immediately, not in ten to fifteen years time.

The government is also banking on Crossrail to lessen the need for additional congestion charge areas around London, as these are very unpopular with the voters and they also reduce levels of trade within their catchments areas. And even more worrying for the Government is that the latest statistics suggest that congestion within the current congestion zone has now returned to pre implementation levels of 2.27 minutes per kilometre. We need to take cars off the road – we all accept that – and the Crossrail project will certainly go some way to achieving this. However, we still need to promote home-working as another alternative because this cost efficient option will have a much greater and more immediate impact. Promoting home-working will also have a nock-on effect on other Government expenditure, such as health, which will definitely benefit from a less stressful and less polluted environment.

Increasing capacity by driving on the hard shoulder of motorways

If Crossrail relates to the downright costly, then this extraordinary proposal comes under the category of the downright dangerous. I use the M25 on a regular basis and I can't believe for one minute that this crazy proposal is going to help. We all know the M25 really needs to be six lanes wide not the three to four lines that it now is, so an additional lane at certain times of the day is not going to help.

Traffic levels on most of our motorways are too high and this tends to lead to unnecessary accidents, which we all know is one of the biggest causes of traffic jams – cars tailing back for miles and miles – and surely these accidents are going to increase further if we remove the safety of the hard shoulder from the equation.

A recent AA research paper suggests that 52 per cent of UK motorists are putting themselves at risk by using the motorway hard shoulder for non-emergency reasons. The latest Department of Transport figures also show that around 170 deaths or serious injuries are caused each year by collisions with cars parked on the hard shoulder. And this is before we start using it as an additional carriageway.

The AA research also highlighted the fact that 17 per cent of motorists are currently unaware of the proper use for the hard shoulder. The top six reasons for pulling onto the hard shoulder are as follows.

1. Taking a toilet break.
2. Checking directions.
3. Using a mobile phone.
4. Attending to children.
5. Waiting for another car when travelling in convoy.
6. Retrieving something from the boot.

If we add to these reasons the legitimate reasons for using the hard shoulder, which are

1. Mechanical breakdown.
2. An emergency (although this can be fairly subjective – how do you quantify what is or isn't an emergency?).

that leaves us with a large number of drivers who use the hard shoulder during the course of their journey. So, are all these drivers suddenly going to change their ways and start to use the hard shoulder sensibly? Well, apparently not. The AA research suggested that nothing was likely to change in the short term as

*   50 per cent of respondents said they would still pull over if a passenger was car sick.
*   34 per cent would pull over to go to the toilet.
*   21 per cent would pull over to use their phone.
*   17 per cent would stop if they were lost to check directions.

So why has the Government decided to use this strategy to try and control the increasing problem of traffic congestion.

1. Hard shoulders can be adapted to cope with traffic in two years, whereas it can take up to ten years to plan and build additional lanes.
2. Costs are expected to be around 80 per cent lower.
3. Introducing motorway tolls will be unpopular with the voters, and will only drive traffic off the motorways and on to small local roads. And taking traffic off these unsuitable roads was of cause the very reason we built motorways in the first place.

Once again there is a much simpler, safer, and more effective way to reach this goal – by positively promoting home-working. This will have an immediate impact on the problem, especially during the peak traffic times.

The increasing population of Britain

According to the Office for National Statistics the British population rose by 10 Million between 1950 and 2000 and is likely to grow to 65.7 million by 2031, before reaching its peak of 67 million two decades later. This means more people commuting to work, clogging our roads and causing greater overcrowding on our trains. If things continue the way they are now we will be doubling our commute time. That's why something needs to change now, and why that change has to be home-working. With the home-working option there are no limiting factors such as space, environmental issues, or increasing costs, which all the other options suffer from. What the Government should do is seriously look at the home-working option now and get a head start on our ballooning population crisis.

13

Health & Safety Executive Guide to Home-Working

As previously stated, even though employees may work from home, their company still has a duty of care towards them in exactly the same way as they do for their office-based staff. In order to help prospective employers to understand their responsibilities to their home-workers I have listed below a brief synopsis of the directive issued by the Health & Safety executive, a full version can be found on their website (www.hse.gov.uk).

What the law requires

The *Health and Safety at Work act 1974 (HSWA)* states that employees have a duty to protect the health, safety and welfare of their employee's, including home-workers. So even though an employee may be working in their own living room, the company still needs to satisfy itself that the working environment meets the legal requirements of the act.

Most of the regulations made under the HSWA apply to home-workers as well as office-based staff. These regulations include the following.

- *The Management of Health and Safety at Work Regulations 1999. (MHSWR)*
- *The Display Screen Equipment Regulations 1992*

97

- *The Manual Handling Operations Regulations 1992*
- *The Provision and Use of Work Equipment Regulations 1998. (PUWER)*
- *The Control of Substances Hazardous to Health Regulations 2002 (as amended). (COSHH)*

Under the *Management of Health and Safety at Work Regulations 1999*, employers are required to do a risk assessment of the work activities carried out by the home-worker. To complete a risk assessment, a trained member of staff needs to visit the employee's home and identify the hazards relating to the home-workers work activities. Having identified these hazards they then need to decide if enough steps have been taken to prevent harm to the home-workers or any one else who may be affected by their work. A risk is defined as the chance, great or small, that someone will be harmed by a hazard, which is defined as anything that may cause harm. Examples of such hazards could be electrical wires that are laid across a walkway, which may cause someone to trip up, poorly maintained electrical equipment, or overloaded power sockets.

How to do a risk assessment

A risk assessment should follow this five-step procedure:

1. Identify any hazards.
2. Decide who might be harmed and how.
3. Assess the risk and take appropriate action to remove them or reduce them as far as possible.
4. Record the findings.
5. Check the risks from time to time and take further steps if needed.

Identifying any hazards

This is the employer's responsibility and not the home-worker's, although we would expect the employee to give serious consideration to this matter – it is after all their health that is at risk. Small hazards should not be ignored as they may still result in harm – for example, keeping potentially harmful substances or equipment out of the reach of children.

Deciding who might be harmed and how

Employers must look at who may be affected by the work done at home and how they may be affected. This will include the home-worker, members of their family, and any visitors.

Assessing the risk and taking appropriate action

When an employer comes across a hazard they need to assess the risk to the home-worker's or anyone else's health and safety in the home, and decide what steps need to be taken to eliminate or reduce those risks as far as possible. The action the employer needs to take depends on the level of the risk, and employers can assess this by looking at what type of harm or injury may arise and how often it may happen. For example, there is a greater risk from loose trailing wires if there are children or elderly people in the home.

In most cases employers can remove the hazard altogether, or reduce the risk to an acceptable level. For example, in the case of the trailing wires, they could be re-routed around the edge of the room and under desks. Most risks can be controlled or overcome simply by using common sense.

If no risks are found to be present then the employer does not need to take any further action, other than periodic checks to ensure that nothing has changed. From my experience, providing common sense is used when setting up the home-working process, this is the most common outcome of the review.

Recording the findings

Employers who have five or more employees, including home-workers, are required by law to record the significant findings from a risk assessment. They need to note down what steps need to be taken and inform the home-workers, or anyone else affected by the work being done, about the findings.

Re-assessing the risk on a regular basis

It is important for employers to regularly check the risk assessment, especially if there is any change in the working environment, such as using a different room as your office, or moving home. This assessment needs to review once again any new hazards that may cause harm to the health or safety of the home-worker, or any other associated people affected by the change in working conditions.

Some common hazards

Some of the common hazards that may be encountered by home-workers are as follows.

- **Moving or storing heavy equipment**
  If heavy equipment needs to be moved the employee should have received adequate training.

- **Trailing or loose wires**
  Set up equipment close to power sockets and make sure wires are routed around the room and not across the main thoroughfare.

- **Overloaded plug sockets**
  Make sure you have enough plug sockets to run your equipment. Use surge protectors to prevent damage to equipment.

100

- **Poorly maintained electrical equipment**
  Make sure all equipment is maintained in good working order and used in accordance with its safety instructions. Replace any frayed electrical cables.

- **Poor lighting**
  We only have one pair of eyes so we need to look after them. Ensure you have adequate lighting, especially if you are using computer screens.

- **Incorrect workstation set-up**
  See the chapter in this book on workstation set-up (Chapter 1). No one needs to suffer from repetitive strain injury if their workstations are set up correctly.

Using work equipment at home

Employees who provide their home-workers with equipment to carry out their work have a duty to ensure that:

- The equipment is correct for the job that is being done.

- Proper information and training is given on how to use the equipment, so that the task can be performed properly and safely. For the use of computer equipment this covers the initial workstation set-up.

- The equipment being used is checked regularly and kept in a condition that does not cause harm to the home-worker or others.

- Those people who are testing the equipment, or training the home-workers, are properly trained themselves; otherwise they cannot provide the correct information and training.

- The machine being used has protective equipment – for example, a machine guard to prevent the home-worker, or anyone else, being injured when it is in use.

- The necessary personal protective equipment is provided for using the equipment safely.

- The equipment has the right controls to allow the work to be undertaken safely, for example, the controls should be clearly marked and properly positioned.

- Checks on the equipment are carried out safely, for example, machines are switched off while being checked.

The *Provision and Use of Work Equipment Regulations 1998* cover the use of work equipment in the home. Guidelines for the use of protective equipment at home are covered by the *Personal Protective Equipment at Work Regulations 1992*.

Using electrical equipment for home-working

If home-workers use electrical equipment provided by the employer as part of their work, the employer is responsible for its maintenance. However, employers are only responsible for the equipment they supply. Electrical sockets, and other parts of the home-workers domestic electrical system are their own responsibility.

Listed below are some simple steps that employs can take to prevent harm or injury to home-workers, or other people, when home-workers use electrical equipment in the home.

- Ensure electrical equipment is turned off before it is checked.

- Check that plugs are not damaged.

- Check the domestic electrical system is adequate for the use of the electrical equipment.

- Check that plugs are correctly wired and maintained.

- Check that the outer covering of the cable or wire is gripped where it enters the plug or the equipment. This will prevent wirers from being pulled loose from their connections, which can be a fire hazard.

- Check that the outer cover of the equipment is not damaged, for example look for loose parts or screws.

- Check leads, wires, or cables for damage to the outer covering.

- Check for burn marks or staining that suggests overheating.

- Repair electrical equipment that may cause harm or injury to the home-worker.

- Last but not least, check that there are no trailing wires. If there are tuck them out of the way.

Just looking for any damage to electrical equipment can prevent most of the faults that can cause harm. The safe use of electricity at work is covered by the *Electricity at Work Regulations 1989*.

Working with VDUs

The use of VDUs is covered by the *Health & Safety (Display Screen Equipment) Regulations 1992*, as amended by the *Health & Safety (Miscellaneous Amendments) Regulations 2002*. Under this regulation employers have a duty to make sure that the display screen equipment used by home-workers is safe and does not affect the user's health.

When working with VDUs it is important for home-workers to adjust their workstation to a comfortable position and take regular breaks from using the VDU. The latter is more of a problem for home-workers as they have fewer interruptions and are therefore more likely to get locked into staring at that screen. Taking regular breaks will help to prevent undue tiredness and eyestrain. Home-workers should also remember to stretch and change position regularly as this will relive tiredness and prevent pains in the hands, wrists, arms, neck, and shoulders or back. VDUs also need to be placed in a position where lighting will not cause reflections or glare on the screen.

It is also important for the home-worker to be able to view the screen comfortably. VDU operators are entitled to free eye tests from their employers, and may need special spectacles for VDU usage.

Here is a checklist of points that employers need to be aware of when their home-workers use VDU's:

- Is the screen clear and readable, and without flicker?

- Is the screen free from glare and reflections?

- Are the brightness and contrast controls properly adjusted to prevent eyestrain?

- Is there suitable lighting so that the fine detail on the screen can be seen and read?

- Is the keyboard placed in the right position to allow the home-worker to work comfortably?

- Is the screen and computer clean: is it free from dust and dirt?

- Can the home-worker's chair be adjusted to the right height so that work can be completed comfortably?

- Is the VDU placed at the right angle on the desk to allow the home-worker to comfortably view the screen while keeping their head at the optimum angle? (See the *A Quick Set-up Guide set out in Chapter 1.*)

- Is there enough space under the desk to allow free movement?

- Is there enough space generally on the desk so that the home-worker can move freely between the work on the desk and the VDU.

New and expectant mothers

New legislation required to implement the *European Directive on Pregnant Workers* was introduced in 1994 and is covered by the *Management of Health and Safety at Work Regulations 1999.*

When assessing risks to the home-worker, the new legislation requires the employer to pay special attention to home-workers who are new or expectant mothers. Risks include those to the unborn child or to the child of a woman who is still breast-feeding – not just risks to the mother herself. A new or expectant mother means a home-worker who is pregnant, who has given birth within the previous six months, or who is breast-feeding.

This is a complicated subject in its own right and as such outside the scope of this book. However, useful guides on this subject can be obtained from the Health & Safety Executive website.

Reporting of Injuries, Disease & Dangerous Occurrences Regulations 1995 (RIDDOR 95)

The revised RIDDOR regulations came into force on the 1st April 1996, and they also apply to home-workers. These regulations place a duty on the employer to report and keep a record of certain work-related accidents, injuries, diseases, and dangerous occurrences. Employers have a duty to ensure that they find out about accidents, injuries, disease, or dangerous occurrences arising from work-related activities – something that is not easy to control with home-workers. Home-workers have to be made aware that they must report any such occurrences.

Health & Safety Executive inspectors

HSE inspectors enforce the *Health and Safety At Work Act (HSWA)* and the regulations made under the HSWA, that apply to home-working. Inspectors visit employees and also have the right to visit home-workers, to ensure that risks from work and working at home are properly managed. They also investigate and help settle complaints about working conditions that could affect the health, safety, or welfare of employees, including home-workers.

Further information

If you have a problem with health and safety, further advice and help is available from:

- Your local HSE office (see under Health and Safety Executive in your local phone book.

- Trade Unions

- Home-workers Helpline Tel: 0800 174095

- National Group on Home-working
  Office 26
  30-38 Dock Street
  Leeds
  LS10 1JF
  Tel: 0800 174095

- Pay and Employment Rights Service
  Field House
  15 Wellington Road
  Dewsbury
  WF13 1HF
  Tel: 01924 439587

14

Sample Contract

When I offered my credit controllers the option of working from home we simply created an amendment to their general terms and conditions of employment. As they had already signed a contract of employment with us, the amendment, which is detailed below, was sufficient to meet our legal requirements. However, as our home-working process develops and we employ people specifically to work from home, then we will need to integrate the home-working clauses into our general employment contract.

The important thing to remember is that a home-working contract does not have to be any more complicated or detailed than your standard terms of employment. As an example of this the amendments I made to our terms and conditions of employment are detailed below.

Centaur Media: Amendment to general terms and conditions of employment for home-based employees

General

1. *As a home-based worker your designated place of work is your home.*

2. *All home-based employees must fulfil the following requirements:*

   a. *All home-based employees must be a homeowner, or have lived at their current address for at least six months.*

   b. *All home-based credit controllers must achieve an average of 50 outgoing calls per day, which are in excess of thirty seconds in duration. The average calls figure will be measured over a rolling ten-day period.*

3. *The hours of employment for home-based employees are 9:30 to 5:30, Monday to Friday, with one hour for lunch.*

4. *For existing office-based credit controllers, there will be a three-month trial period before any home-based role is made permanent. During this period either party can revoke the agreement and return to a normal office-based role.*

5. *Credit controllers who are employed specifically in a home-based role, will still be subject to the Company's normal three-month probationary period, of which the first month must be worked in the office. However, there is no automatic right of transfer to an office-based role.*

6. *No more than two home-based workers will be allowed to take holidays at the same time, unless the Group Credit Manager specifically gives permission.*

Equipment

1. *On occasions when equipment failure renders home-based working impossible, the Company reserves the right to request all home-based workers to attend the office until the fault is rectified.*

2. *Home-workers must co-operate with all reasonable requests from the company to enter their home to carry out safety checks, or the repair or removal of Company equipment. The Company will normally give a minimum of 48 hours notice.*

3. *On leaving the employment of Centaur Media Ltd, the Company has the right to remove its equipment before the expiry of your notice period. You may be requested to work your notice period from the office.*

4. *The cost of the Broadband installation, the line rental charge, and the cost of work related calls are the responsibility of the Company. Private calls should be made on your own private subscriber line. Costs for the additional use of electricity, heating, and general subsistence costs, are the employees responsibility*

5. *Use of the 24-hour Internet facility will be subjected to the Company's normal Internet usage policy.*

6. *Any equipment installed within your home remains the sole property of Centaur Media Ltd, and must be operated within the Company's standard terms of use.*

Health & Safety

1. *The Company's health and safety guidelines will apply to the office in your home, and must be followed in full. Special attention should be made to the overloading of electrical sockets, trailing loose wires across the floor, and the ergonomic set-up of your computer screen and keyboard. The I.T.*

department will ensure the correct set-up of your computer during installation.

2. It is the employee's responsibility to ensure their building insurance company have been informed that they will be working from home, and that this does not adversely affect their buildings or contents cover.

3. During the probationary period, all home-based workers will be required to attend the office once a week to assess their progress. The frequency of these debriefing sessions may be altered on the agreement of both parties, but only once the probationary period has been successfully completed.

4. All other Terms and Conditions of Employment remain as set out in the Centaur Staff Handbook.

To indicate your acceptance of these terms and conditions please sign and date in the space provided below.

------------------------------------   ------------------------------------

Date_____   Date_____

xxxxxxxxxx (Employee)   *Alan Dixie FICM*
Head of Accounting Services

Public sector, local government and utilities

Although some of the staff at Centaur Media have union representation, we are not a heavily unionised company, but for organisations such as Local Councils, Utilities, or rail companies this will not be the case. In these instances union representation will be sought as part of the process of developing a home-working contract. As a result of union liaison these types of home-working contracts will be more detailed in their content as can be seen from the extracts below.

County Council terms of employment

A number of changes in County Council terms of employment have been made to incorporate home-based working:

- *Many staff will be able to work anywhere, including their home, and at any time. To complement this change, the terms and conditions of service will be modernised to allow employees flexible working by removing the constraints of time and place of work, or tightly defined job descriptions, from their contracts of employment. Each employee, and manager, will undergo new skills training and development in order to take full advantage of the new arrangements.*

- *A cross-departmental working committee will be set up and meet fortnightly, which will look at the home-working process and how to develop the process to bring even greater benefits to the employer, employee, and the customer.*

- *Home-based working requires the consent of both employee and line manager.*

- *Home-based workers have an administrative centre, which they must attend regularly.*

- *Managers have a responsibility to ensure that home-workers receive information and communication.*

- *Normally there will be no change in contractual hours, but the pattern of work hours is to be agreed between the employer and employee.*

- *The home-based employee's manager is responsible for arranging a risk assessment in the employee's home.*

- *Home equipment for work is provided and maintained by the employer.*

- *The employer may seek access to an employee's home; normally reasonable notice will be given. Reasons for attendance to an employee's home will include, routine maintenance of equipment, health and safety assessments, and in some cases urgent maintenance or health and safety purposes.*

- *There will be arrangements for travel allowance, travel expenses, and subsistence.*

- *The employer will install an additional phone line, and pay for the installation, line rental, and work related calls.*

- *Employees will be paid a home-based working allowance to compensate them for the cost of providing a workspace at home.*

Other companies' contracts

I have listed below extracts from home-working contracts drawn up by a large telecommunications company, a large gas supplier, and a bank, which you may find useful when drawing up your own home-working contracts.

The telecommunication contract

- *There will be no change to pay, hours of work, annual leave entitlement, or superannuation arrangements, unless specifically stated in this contract.*

- *Home-workers will continue to receive details of job opportunities, general notices, etc., and may apply and be considered for posts on an equal basis with office-based staff.*

- *Appraisals, counselling and training processes will continue to apply for home-based workers.*

- *A home-based worker's place of work will be their home, although it will be necessary to visit the office on a regular basis, for which reasonable travelling expenses will be reimbursed in accordance with existing travel and subsistence conditions.*

- *The company will provide a separate telephone line and will meet the costs of rental and work related call charges. Any other equipment required to work from home will be supplied by the company and will at all times remain the property of the company.*

- *The company will pay for the insurance of all company equipment used at the home. The home-based employee should ensure that their building/contents insurance(s) are not invalidated by the use of the home as a place of work, or the storage of company equipment.*

- *The company and the home-based employee share joint legal responsibility under the **Health and Safety at Work Act 1974**, to ensure that the part of the employers home which is used as their place of work is at all times maintained in a safe condition.*

- *The company is seeking to agree tax allowances with the Inland Revenue for heating and lighting costs.*

- *Visits to the home of the home-based employee will be necessary, before, during, and after completion of a period of home-working. Access to the home will only be undertaken with the express permission of the home-worker.*

- *It is the home-worker's responsibility to ensure that work is completed properly and securely in accordance with the standards that would apply in the office.*

The gas supplier's contract

- *Employees should be reimbursed financially for all additional expenses incurred as a result of home-working, but should not financially benefit from the reimbursement.*

- *Home-working offers advantages to the individual in planning and managing in a flexible manner their work and personal time. Therefore within the context of completing their required working hours, home-workers may wish to adjust their working hours where on a daily basis this primarily meets business needs and personal circumstances.*

- *Employees should ensure that relevant bodies (insurance companies, local councils etc) are notified in writing of the change to home-based working.*

- *The company will meet all the installation costs for equipping the employee to work from home. This will include the cost of necessary modifications and making good any disturbance to the home decor.*

- *Equipment will be sited at the employee's preference in the home, provided that this does not interfere with the proper operation of the equipment, and also meets Health & Safety requirements.*

- *The company will meet all additional running costs associated through working from home. This will include the cost of operating equipment and any additional heating and lighting costs.*

- *The company will pay for any additional insurance premiums an employee incurs as a result of working from home, or having the company's equipment in the home.*

- *The company will ensure that employees are made aware of the possible implication of home-working for their tenancy or mortgage agreements before the commencement of home-working. The company will meet any additional costs incurred as a result.*

- *The company will also advise its employees on the tax implications and benefits of home-working. However, it should be remembered that matters of taxation are the responsibility of the individual employee with the Inland Revenue.*

The bank's contract

- *Line Management, in conjunction with Human Resources, will be responsible for assessing the suitability of home-working. Selection criteria will be based on the suitability of the premises, relevant and recent experience in the role, and personal characteristics deemed to be selection absolutes. Selection will be judged against competencies and criteria that have been identified as key to be able to work productively and competently in the home environment.*

- *Where practicable, current working patterns will be reviewed with a view to increased flexibility of working hours to meet the employee's personal circumstances whilst continuing to meet business requirements.*

- *The home-based worker's place of work will be their current address. Should they wish to move to a new property, then the suitability of those premises will need to be assessed, and home-working will only continue with the banks expressed agreement.*

- *The bank has agreed with the Inland Revenue an adjustment to the home-worker's PAYE code to cover any reasonable household expenses such as heating and lighting, which arise from home-working. Tax relief will be received on the following amounts. Full time staff £300 per annum. Part time staff £150 per annum.*

- *The bank will provide the agreed equipment for the home-worker, and will be responsible for its instillation and maintenance, as well as repair and removal, and all necessary stationery.*

- *It is recognised that home-based workers may feel a sense of isolation; therefore to counter this, line managers will continue to involve home-workers in regular team meetings. Line managers will also ensure that daily contact is made with the home-worker from office-based staff. Home-workers will also be part of any published team/departmental organisation structures.*

- *Trade Union representation arrangements will continue to apply as for office-based staff.*

- *The home will be surveyed by a representative of the Bank's Group Property Department to asses whether it is suitable for the purpose of home-working against Health & Safety standards.*

- *During the selection process the home will also be surveyed by a qualified electrician, which will be paid for by the bank. Should work be required to ensure that an acceptable safety standard is obtained, the home-worker will be responsible for this cost.*

15

Conclusions

There is no doubt that home-working does offer solutions to some of the most pressing problems that we face today. Today's manic lifestyle and its incessant demand for consumer products, has increased the pressure placed upon the individual to succeed. This has resulted in a massive increase in work related stress, a situation that is costing commerce billions of pounds each year through absenteeism and reduced productivity. Home-based working cuts through the problem of work related stress, by offering employees greater control over their working environment, and delivering a better work-life balance.

Home-based working would also bring about an instant reduction in the level of traffic congestion that is hampering the commercial growth of our metropolitan cities. At present we annually travel 78.5 billion miles commuting to work, and a further 43.8 billion business related miles. As our population grows – and present forecasts suggest it will peak at 67 million – these figures will increase further. This means we need to take drastic action now if we are to prevent total gridlock. We all have to accept that something is wrong if it was quicker to travel around London by horse and cart than it is by today's modern forms of transport. London's congestion charge may be raising large sums of revenue, but it is having a detrimental effect on trade within the congestion charge area, and is doing little, if anything, to improve the congestion problem. Crossrail, if it finally gets of the ground, will help, but the benefits will not be seen until ten years from now, by which time our ever-increasing population will have negated its benefit and we will be back to square one.

The answer to the congestion problem is quite simple. We need to reduce the number of people commuting to work and the number of business journeys undertaken each year. Combining home-working with the benefits of tele-conferencing can fulfil this requirement. All we need is for the Government to encourage use of home-working, and this could simply be achieved through offering tax relief to companies who implement home-working projects. This would lead to an instant growth in the level of home-working, and we would quickly see substantial benefits to our road and rail congestion problem.

As the Government struggles with the complex issues of emission control, and meeting its targets to reduce greenhouse gases, I am sure the benefits of home-working will slowly dawn upon them. Developing wind farms, harnessing wave power, building new homes with zero carbon footprints – all of these things will help, but on their own they will not achieve the goals we set ourselves. What we need is a process that will take numerous cars, buses and trains out of the equation. Then and only then will we get anywhere near to achieving our goals.

The other major benefit of home-working will be the reduction of work-related stress, which currently accounts for a third of all new incidences of ill health. Stress-related illnesses have increased significantly over the last two decades, and home-based working is the ideal way to reverse this trend. This will not only benefit the employer by increasing productivity; it will also offer the employee a healthier work-life balance. Controlling stress levels will also reduce the financial burden that stress-related illness places on the National Health Service, which currently runs at approximately £2.5 billion a year. All of these things have got to be good for the employer, the employee, and the environment in which we live.

Since instigating home-working, my company, Centaur Media, has achieved benefits way beyond our original expectations.

Hopefully, having read this book, you will accept that working from home is not a skiver's paradise – and understand why I said that I am serious about home-working, and that it really does work. Home-working offers a better and more secure future for us all, so please step aboard and enjoy the journey of a lifetime.

Index

Absenteeism, 24

British Telecom Survey, 87
Broadband, 13

Carbon footprint, 35
Community, 37
Commuting cost, 27
Competition, 68
Computer set-up, 15
Contracts, 107–20
County Councils, 112
Crossrail, 92

Earning potential, 33
Equipment, 101
Equipment maintenance, 40
Ergonomics, 17

Fax, 15

Goal-setting, 63
Greenhouse gases, 36

Health and safety, 17, 37,
    97–106
    risk assessment, 98
Healthy lifestyle, 33

Managing home-workers,
    39–43

Maslow's motivational
    categories, 47

Obsolete Office Survey, 83
Office-based support, 41
Overhead reduction, 26

Performance measurement,
    53–60
Performance targets, 42
Printers, 17
Productivity, 22

Security, 47
Self esteem, 48
Self-development, 48
Staff retention, 27
Starfax, 15
Stress, 33
Survey
    British Telecom, 87
    Obsolete Office, 83

Targets, 55
Team spirit, 69
Traffic improvement, 37
Travelling time and costs, 29

Workflow control, 40
Working hours, 61
Work-life balance, 32